CHATSWORTH
PRESS

THE CRITICS AND PROFESSIONALS COMMENT ON

TOUCHING FOR PLEASURE

THE BOOK:

". . . a well-written, beautifully illustrated exercise in the lost art of tactile pleasure . . ."[1]

". . . many titles extoll the virtues of touch and sexual sensitivity, few actually give detailed exercises on how to achieve and increase sensations."[2]

"Here's a book that transcends the boundaries of conventional massage techniques — touching for its own reward is the highest form of massage. **TOUCHING FOR PLEASURE** presents simple exercises that provide much of the benefit of traditional massage, but the goal of this book is a deeper understanding of our bodies and an enhanced communication between people."[3]

FEAR OF TOUCHING:

"Now a book that's made me sit and think . . . we've all known persons who fear touching or being touched. I've known two marriages that broke up on this hidden rock. Perhaps those involved were too fearful to know they needed touching. Some of us fear many things we need — sometimes love itself."[4]

"Many adults never receive the warmth and affection experienced as children or infants. Without this connection with others there is an emotional and physical emptiness that is constantly needing fulfillment."[5]

TOUCHING AND GUILT:

"Most of us feel guilty when on the 'receiving end' of pleasure, feeling as though we must reciprocate . . . you will be taught to pay attention to your own pleasure . . . the reciprocity will be automatic!"[6]

Reviews are continued on page 120.

1) Marylin March, THE BOOK REVIEW; 2) Diane C. Donovan, THE BOOKWATCH;
3) Leonard Jacobs, EAST WEST MAGAZINE: 4) William Hill, THE BOOK REPORT;
5) Jacobs; 6) March.

Masters & Johnson Human Sex Response Chart used by permission.

Though all the exercises mentioned in this publication are simple and do not require physical exertion, it is always wise to consult a physician to determine your ability to participate in the program.

Cover Design by Scott S. Brastow
Ms. Dean Photographed by Tim Dressler
Ms. Kennedy Photographed by Robin Robin
Illustrations © 1986, 1988 Joann Daley

Published in the United States of America by
Chatsworth Press, 9135 Alabama Avenue, Suite B, Chatsworth, CA 91311
Second Edition
Library of Congress Catalog Number 85 62992
ISBN 0-917181-11-5
Printed in the United States of America
15   14   13   12   11   10   9

TOUCHING
for pleasure

A 12 STEP PROGRAM
FOR
SEXUAL ENHANCEMENT

By Adele P. Kennedy
and
Susan Dean, Ph.D.

Illustrated by Joann Daley

CHATSWORTH PRESS

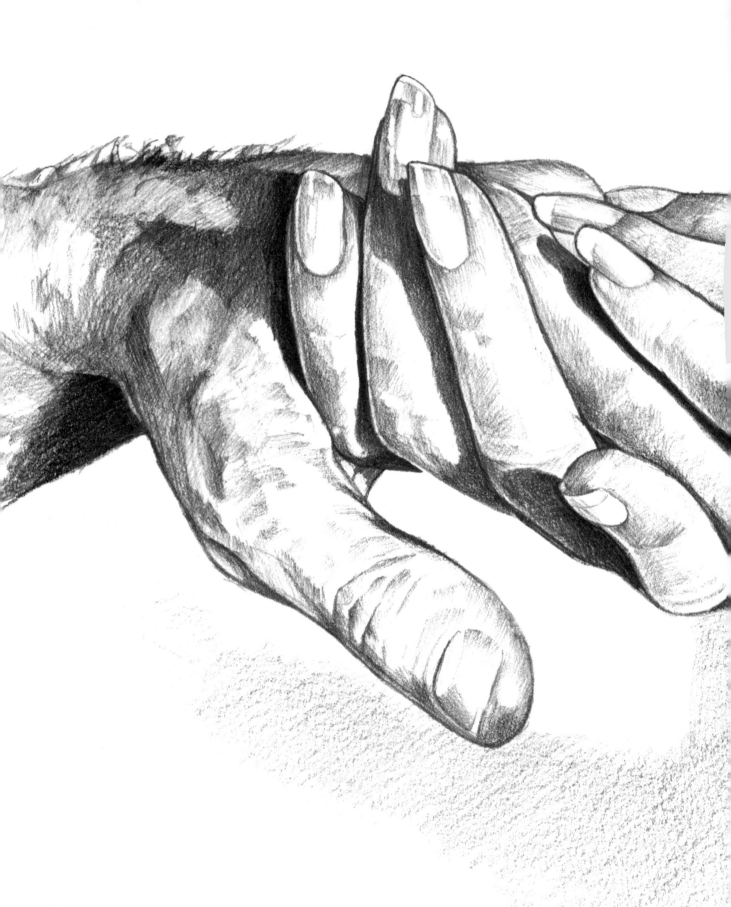

. . . for JoEmily, Edward, Joelle, and Justin

Adele Kennedy is one of the pioneers in the sex surrogate field and has worked in conjunction with medical professionals for more than a decade. She has taught hundreds of people to rebuild their socio-sexual confidence and skills, and has made them aware of their potential for physical gratification. Ms. Kennedy has run workshops for sex therapists, surrogate trainees and for women's groups, and has acted as consultant to publishers, authors, and documentary film makers. She has been actively involved in human sexuality organizations such as: Association of Sex Educators, Counselors, and Therapists; Society for the Scientific Study of Sex; and International Professional Surrogates Association. In 1981 Ms. Kennedy became a fellow of the Masters and Johnson Institute, and in 1985 she was listed in the Who's Who of Sexology. She practices and resides in Los Angeles, California.

Susan Dean holds a doctorate in Behavioral Science and has been researching and writing in the field of human sexuality for the past ten years. Her work has included a nationwide survey of women done in conjunction with a study of female sexuality which she began while at UCLA in the mid-seventies. Ms. Dean has lectured since that time to psychology and sociology students at California State University, utilizing the classroom as a forum for disseminating information and eliciting data. She conducted extensive research for Sensory Research Corporation, collecting product information and consumer response. Ms. Dean has written several magazine articles and short stories, all of which focus on sensual and sexual enhancement. For the past thirteen years she has made her home in Los Angeles, California.

Susan Perry has a masters degree in Human Development, and she has been an independent writer for nine years. Her articles appear in *USA Today*, the *Los Angeles Times*, and regional and specialized publications. Her areas of specialty include family, psychological, educational, and sexual topics. She lives in Los Angeles, California.

ABOUT THE AUTHORS

With deep gratitude we want to thank our publisher, Scott Brastow, for believing in us. To our editor, Jenny Gumpertz, much appreciation for her enthusiasm and willingness to join the team and make it better. And very special thanks to Joann Daley, whose brilliant art work and aesthetic sense made our words come to life.

A big thank you to all the many sex therapists and surrogates, clients, students, and friends who have contributed to and supported the ideals and values set forth in this book.

And finally, we are warmed and pleased by all of you who have permitted yourselves to be touched by us through the pages of this book.

A.K.
S.D.

Through our individual pursuits and exposures, we are both of the same mind regarding sexual fulfillment. In order for a person's sexual capabilities to be fully realized, sensuality must be addressed.

As a way of increasing sexual responsiveness, we have devised a program based on touching as a key principle in pleasuring. It is our belief that when sexual agendas are eliminated and replaced by sensual awareness, performance anxiety and other self-imposed obstacles are reduced accordingly.

This book is the compilation of our professional and personal experiences. It is intended for anyone who enjoys feeling good and has room to feel better.

A.K.
S.D.

For purposes of clarity and continuity we have chosen to use the feminine gender in addressing the reader. This simply avoids the tedium of using he/she or the impersonal it. This book is for both male and female readers and we have made every effort to convey that through the structure of the contents.

All the anecdotes in the text are taken from the authors' personal and professional experiences. To protect the privacy of those individuals wishing anonymity, situations and distinguishing characteristics have been disguised.

TOUCHING
for pleasure

TOUCH STARVED

1

The need for bonding remains with us throughout our lifetime

From the moment of birth our tactile sense is being stimulated. Pushed out, picked up, slapped on the bottom, we are placed at our mother's breast, and a bonding process begins.

The need for bonding, or close physical contact with another human being, remains with us throughout our lifetime. Some of us repress our craving for warmth and affection, while others go to extremes to obtain it. Much of how we function as adults depends on how we were nurtured during infancy.

No one is exempt from needing to be touched. We have all experienced moments when the touch of a hand on our shoulder or a reassuring hug was all that was needed to reduce our fear, anxiety, or loneliness. Touching is an act of love, a way of communicating without words.

Ideally we touch and are touched from birth to death, but unfortunately this is not always the case. We are all plagued, to a certain degree, by social and familial conditioning from our early childhood. As children we were curious to touch everything we saw. But frequently as our hands reached out to explore, an adult voice could be heard to say, "Don't touch," followed by an assortment of reasons implying that touching could be dangerous, rude, disrespectful, shameful, unsanitary, and even sinful.

Many of us have been taught, either openly or by example, that touching is prurient in nature and as such is something to be suspicious of and avoided. This kind of ingrained thinking is often responsible for the sexual dysfunctions we experience as adults. These constraints are difficult to shed, further inhibiting us from natural physical contact with others.

All too often we become embarrassed by accidental touching, especially in public. Even an innocent handshake, if too prolonged, can be misconstrued as an invitation to a sexual encounter. Because touching has an excess of negative associations, with very little provocation it seems we flee from intimacy.

Certain other cultures are less inhibited about touching. For example, in the Soviet Union, as in Latin countries, men openly embrace in public. Americans have a more difficult time accepting open exchange of affection between heterosexual males.

Women are generally freer about hugging each other and holding hands. But if a woman is naturally demonstrative with men, her behavior can be easily misunderstood. Traditionally, a woman is taught to control any display of affection that could be interpreted as sexual; except with her partner. Being a good girl has remained an underlying symbol of Americana.

It would be wonderful if we could all have a second chance to undo our earlier days when all of this negative imprinting began. When we compare our society with others and their treatment of the young, we begin to understand why we have progressed so slowly in tactile communication. We prop our babies in infant seats, balancing their bottles in their mouths; whereas in other countries babies are strapped to their mothers in such a way that the breast is accessible at all times.

The American infant is frequently amused by music, video, and other gadgetry, instead of being held and caressed by human hands.

For our infants' sleep problems we have been equally inventive. Pacifiers, wind-up swings, and medication can quiet the most restless child. Yet comforting arms and body caresses would be more effective than the most sophisticated mechanical equipment.

In the adolescent years, the parents and child begin to withdraw from one another; the teenager out of a sense of self-consciousness with her new feelings and physical changes, and the parents out of book-learned attitudes and discomfort with their developing offspring.

Hugging, kissing, and physical closeness may diminish or stop completely then, leaving the young adult starved for affection. This hunger is often satiated through indiscriminate sex with peers; a way of continuing the touching where the parents left off.

Unfortunately, we cannot go back to the beginning, but we can improve upon the present. Although cultural attitudes toward touching are still restrictive, we can attempt to transcend the dogma that has colored

TOUCH STARVED

our ability and willingness to be touched, and eradicate touch starvation from our lives.

Touching for pleasure is a concept that returns you to a guileless level of innocence and purity, where the imprinting and limits that have obstructed your pleasure are removed. The purpose of this book and its program is to reacquaint you with your sensual responses. Through tactile stimulation your skin will begin to wake up to its own sensuality. The cutaneous connection between two people is perhaps the most intimate of all human exchange.

In fact, the skin is the largest sex organ of our bodies. Even the skin of the hands and feet, when gently touched, can send stimuli toward the genital area,

causing sexual interest to begin. The response that begins on the surface of the skin moves inward, and the sexual energy is brought into focus. The arousal from a skin caress may be so subtle at first that you are unaware of the slow, steady buildup of sexual feelings.

Sexual responsiveness is not a primary goal of learning to touch for pleasure. It can, however, be a natural outgrowth of touching. Later in the book we will discuss sexual attitudes and activities. But the main focus of this program is to awaken your physical senses by teaching you to touch with care and to enrich your life with your new sensual awareness.

Sensual, as we use it in this book, means tuning in to the pleasure of touching the skin on various parts of the body. *Sexual* means the involvement of the genital area, including the responses associated with sexual activity. Clearly, sensuality and sexuality are not mutually exclusive.

Once you have learned how to touch with sensual gratification, other opportunities for pleasure will open up to you. Being in control of your body is a step toward personal freedom. Touching for pleasure broadens your options and ultimately brings you great rewards.

We have divided our touch program into ten steps. It is structured for either sex, any age group, the single or partnered, and any sexual persuasion. Our intent is to offer you—no matter who you are and what your situation is—a way to rediscover yourself through touch.

This book, like the program, is a process. It is important that you read the chapters in sequence and do the exercises in the same order as the chapters. If you skip over one part of the program or perform it out of order, the thrust of the program changes. When you have followed the program through once completely in order, you can reread any chapter or portion as a reference or guide. Whether you are studying alone or with another person, plan to experience only one exercise—one chapter—at a time. That is, do the hand caress the first time. Then study the face caress the second time. And so forth.

When you are ready to begin your journey, we ask that you follow certain guidelines in order to give yourself every opportunity for success.

To begin with, create an environment that is conducive to concentration and pleasure by eliminating as many distractions as possible. Turn off the television, radio, and telephone. Don't even answer the door. This is your time to feel good. We ask that you avoid sharing it with anyone except your chosen partner.

Wear comfortable clothes and remove all jewelry. Find a soft couch or a bed on which both of you can sit as you begin your caress exercises. As you progress with the program and become more proficient at focusing and in the touching itself, it will be less necessary to control your surroundings. It takes time and practice to learn how to stay concentrated in the moment, but it can be done.

If you are sharing the exercises with another person, decide who will first take the active role. If you are the one who starts out as the active partner, then finish in the passive role. Allow a minimum of one hour for two-person exercises, thirty minutes in each role.

The main thing to remember in practicing these exercises is to pay attention to your own pleasure, whether you are in the active or passive role. Your partner is to do the same, to focus on his own pleasure. This is difficult for most of us to do at first. As an active partner, you are probably used to worrying about what you can do to please the other person. And as a passive partner, at a certain point you tend to cut off your feelings and think that you have been touched long enough. You feel guilty about being on the receiving end for too long. You've been taught that this is selfish. You force yourself to respond to an imaginary timer that alerts you when your time for good feelings is up, and instructs you to return the favor. But responding to this timer will sabotage your pleasure.

What you will come to understand through these exercises is that once you learn how to accept pleasure, the need to pay it back will disappear and you will be giving pleasure as you receive it. The reciprocity is automatic. For although you are concerned with your own feelings, you are aware of your partner's responses as well. Do the exercises very slowly, so that you can be fully conscious of what you are feeling and discovering with your partner.

TOUCH STARVED

What occurs in the process is a give-and-take, an exchange of pleasure. This mutuality enhances all your sensual and sexual experiences greatly. Whether in the active or passive role, let your body flow with its feelings. In this way you allow all your senses to become sharper. Your benefits increase. As your partner learns to do the same, you both experience the best and highest degree of satisfaction. The very fact that you are in a positive state of mind makes the interaction a more equitably pleasing one. Your sense of well-being and good feelings about yourself and the gratification you feel will become contagious and soon your partner will be sharing in your response.

There is a natural tendency to want to converse with your partner during the exercises, but try to avoid communication in the beginning, either by words or gestures. In all of the exercises, stay in your assigned role, either completely active or completely passive. Once you have silently completed the first half hour, then discuss your feelings about the experience. After switching roles and performing the exercise again, once more verbalize your feelings. Each chapter contains guidelines for the appropriate sharing in the exercise.

Nondefensive communication is important to the success of your pleasuring experience. Rapport between you and your partner is essential. The giving of and listening for personal information plays an important part in learning how to touch and be touched.

People are inclined to respond defensively when they are told by a partner what to do and how to do it. Be sensitive to each other's feelings when you talk about what brings each of you the greatest amount of pleasure. If you do the exercises again with the same or another partner, remember that pleasure differs from one time to another. Talking about preferences and feelings eliminates guesswork and removes possible obstacles born out of confusion, fear, and anxiety.

Having talked about your experiences together, you and your partner will find yourselves touching with more interest as the exercises progress. You will be absorbed in what you are touching and how it feels to you. When you simply experience the touching, your partner becomes aware of the attention you are paying him. This encourages his responsiveness. The greater the experience is for both of you, the more likely you will want to continue learning to touch for pleasure.

Each time you and your partner meet, the encounter is brand new. Moods and sensitivities change; physical conditions change. Approach touching without any preconceived expectations and the reward for both you and your partner will be greater.

Remember you are not trying to reach any particular goal as you touch. When you are goal-oriented you are no longer in the present. You interrupt your responses when you try to anticipate the next step.

Stay focused on the moment, so that you receive all that is being offered. Touch is, in and of itself, the pleasure. Any by-product is coincidental to the experience, although it is to be enjoyed and appreciated. The motivation is to sensitize your body to its intrinsic capacity for pleasure.

The most significant aspect of this program is enjoyment. You are about to have an adventure that has been created with your satisfaction in mind. Take advantage of this wonderful opportunity to experience pleasure on all levels. Then extend this new sensitivity into all aspects of your life. Whether you are petting a dog, stroking your child, or caressing your lover, it will be with a greater perception of what it feels like to touch slowly and with interest—to touch for pleasure.

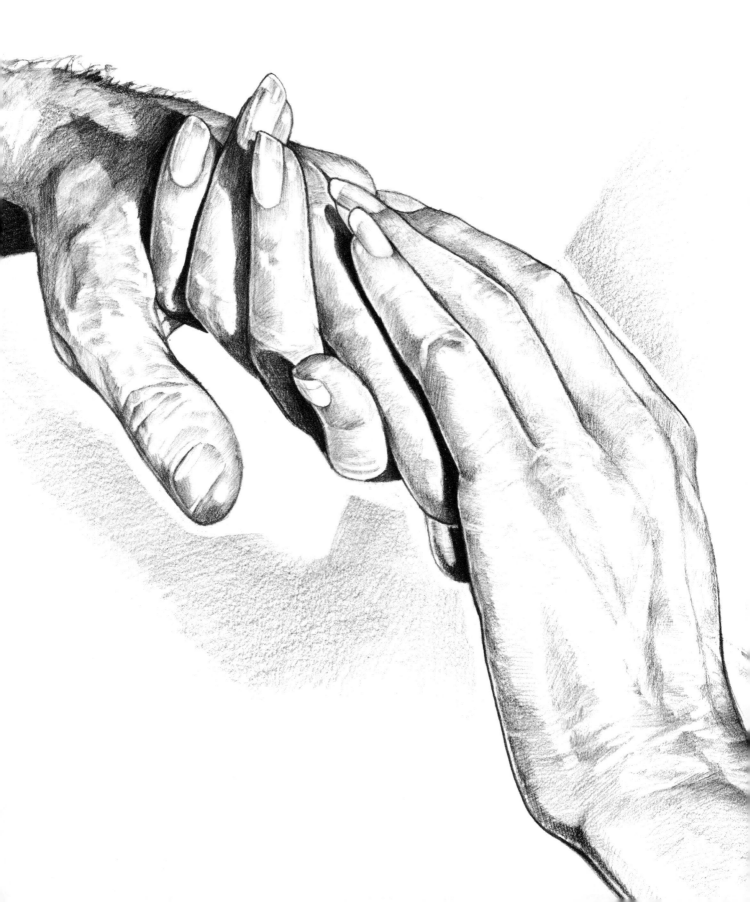

HAND CARESS

In 1976, a study was done at Purdue University to investigate the effects of touch on a random group of students. Clerks at the library were instructed to lightly touch the hand of every other person checking out books, maintaining contact for about half a second.

Upon leaving the building, each person was stopped by a researcher and asked to evaluate the library and describe his feelings about the clerks and himself. All of the men and women whose hands had just barely been touched responded enthusiastically with respect to the facilities and the clerks. They also reported more positive feelings about themselves than the students who had not been touched. Women who had been touched generally rated the library more favorably than did the other women or any of the men. Members of the untouched group were more likely to voice mild complaints and suggestions on how to improve the quality of the library.

The students who had been touched were then told about the experiment. In many cases, they did not recall any extra tactile experience. Subconsciously, however, they had been affected in a positive way.

The starting point for your sensual touching experience is the hand caress. The hand is an appropriate choice for the first exercise because it is the part of the body that tends to show the least resistance to touching, and in fact often welcomes it. A hand is frequently extended as a gesture of friendship or good faith and is generally considered a relatively safe offering between individuals, even upon initial meeting.

2

In the touching of hands there is much to be learned about a person's feelings

In the touching of two hands there is much to be learned about a person's feelings and thoughts, simply through the quality of the contact. A limp handshake feels very different from the grip of a firm hand; they project different sentiments.

Since the early part of the touch program is designed for the use of both the partnered and the unpartnered, we will begin by describing the hand caress exercise for two people, followed by exercises to be done alone.

If you are the partner starting out in the active role, remember that you will be concentrating all your attention on the palms of your hands. Your partner will focus on the area of his hand where you are touching it. Just before your hands actually touch, be aware of the heat between your hands and his. When you touch, concentrate on sending warmth to establish a connection and flow between you. With mutual and total concentration, both your hands and your partner's will become one entity.

To begin, pick up your partner's hand gently, as if it were delicate porcelain; do not release it again until the exercise is over. The passive hand remains limp and does not assist in any way. With eyes closed, the passive partner follows the movements of your fingers or hands as they are caressing. You are keeping your head, heart, soul, emotions, and entire being fixed on your own hands. You are both letting yourselves experience the full impact of your feelings. Reject outside sound and other disturbances and maintain a state of concentration. If you become distracted by intruding thoughts, immediately bring your attention back to what you are doing. Focus on where you are touching, or where you are being touched.

As the active partner, you are exploring your partner's hand for every fold, crease, and ridge, constantly keeping your own pleasure in mind as you do so. Remember, there is no pressure to perform or please.

With your fingertips, trace the hills and valleys of your partner's hand. Lightly glide along the edge of the palm. As you slide in between each finger, feel its thickness as well as the thickness of the skin. What are the nails like? Are they long or short? Is the skin warm or cool? Is it smooth or chafed? During this process of light caressing, don't be concerned with your partner's reactions. Focus strictly on your own sensations as you discover the unique qualities of another hand, totally unlike your own.

As you both become more comfortable with the situation, close your own eyes so that you don't have to deal with the "noise" of looking. You will discover how much more intensely feelings come through. Fix

all your attention on the wonderful impressions you're getting from the hand you are holding. You and your partner are each experiencing different sensations in the active and passive roles, but because you are both feeling, this is true mutuality. And remember to be silent. Conversation detracts from the special quality of the moment.

Be aware that you must go slowly so that no portion of the process is missed. If you hurry, you severely limit the delightful sensations to be had. It is much like slowing down your automobile to 25 mph, as opposed to hurtling along at three times the speed. You can see a lot more from the slower car.

In caressing the skin of the hand or any other part of the body, proceed lightly as well as slowly. Pressing down firmly pushes on muscle tissue. We are not interested in massaging the muscles. It is the nerve tissue we want to stimulate. If the pressure is too firm those particular nerves will not be activated. A caress is all that is needed to produce sensation. The whole body is sensitive to very light touch. If you touch the hair at its outermost ends, you might expect there would be no feeling. But every hair has a root, and every root has a nerve. You don't have to press down at all. Just touch the hair ends, and the nerves respond.

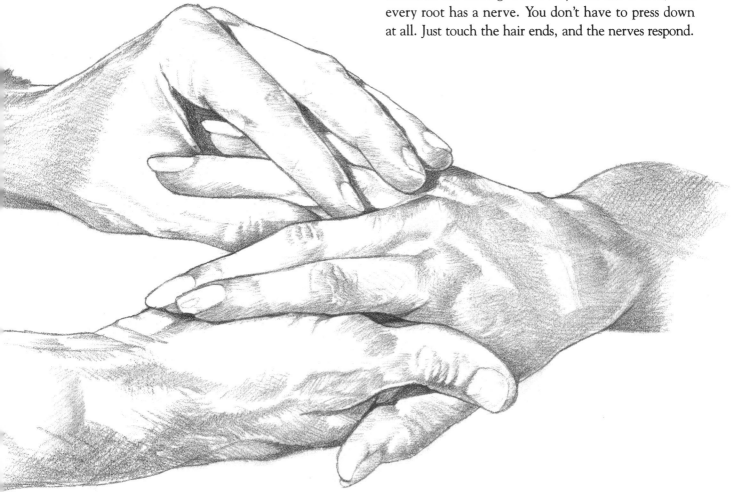

This is why you want to caress and not massage. The pressure of massage is likely to numb the skin.

If during the exercise one of you finds that a particular kind of touch, or touch in a particular area, is uncomfortable or unpleasant, let your partner know. Try to do it in a nonverbal way. Shift into a more comfortable position, or gently guide your partner's hand away from the uncomfortable area. Sometimes an enthusiastic lover rubs one spot so hard or so long that the nerves deaden. Use nice, long, slow strokes, without moving the flesh. This kind of touch magnifies sensual feelings.

After you have fully caressed and explored your partner's hand, do the same with his other hand. Spend about half an hour on the total process. Then it is time to stop and discuss what you are learning about yourselves and each other.

Now is the time for conversation, before you switch roles for the second half of the exercise. You can't be expected to know or feel what another person likes or dislikes, so it is to your mutual advantage to hear it expressed. Tell each other as much as you can about your impressions and feelings. Avoid words such as *wonderful, nice, fabulous, awful,* or *terrible.* These are verbal shortcuts that do not tell the whole story. Use more specific terms, such as *hot, cold, hard, soft, gentle, ticklish,* or *painful* to make your meaning clear. This minimizes the possibility of incorrect assumptions.

Tact is important in describing your sensual adventure. This conversation is a learning experience, not a critique. It is merely the relating of factual information. Do not take anything said personally.

Now it is time for you to take the passive role. Relax and let your partner gently touch and experience each of your hands, as you focus on the pleasure of your response. After about half an hour, stop and talk about your experiences in your new role. You have now completed the hand caress exercise with a partner.

It is also important to study the hand caress alone, without a partner. Doing touching exercises by yourself is great practice, because being alone allows for greater concentration.

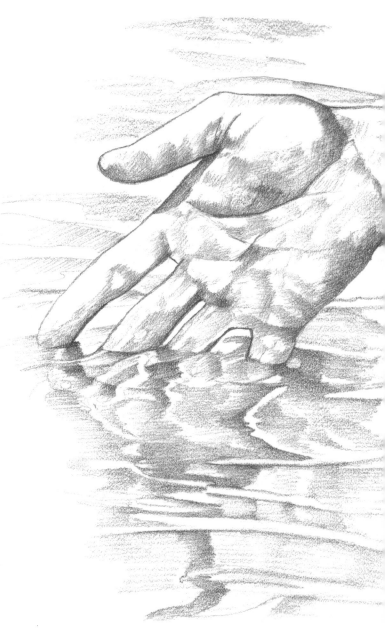

Touch everything inanimate you can find around the house. Feel the scratches and dents of an old wooden table, the coolness and smoothness of a mirror. Dig into the dirt of a flowerpot. Lightly press your palms against a window that's been heated by the sun's rays.

Glide your hands into a basin of warm water. Gently move your hands back and forth a fraction of an inch, without making a ripple. Let the water caress them.

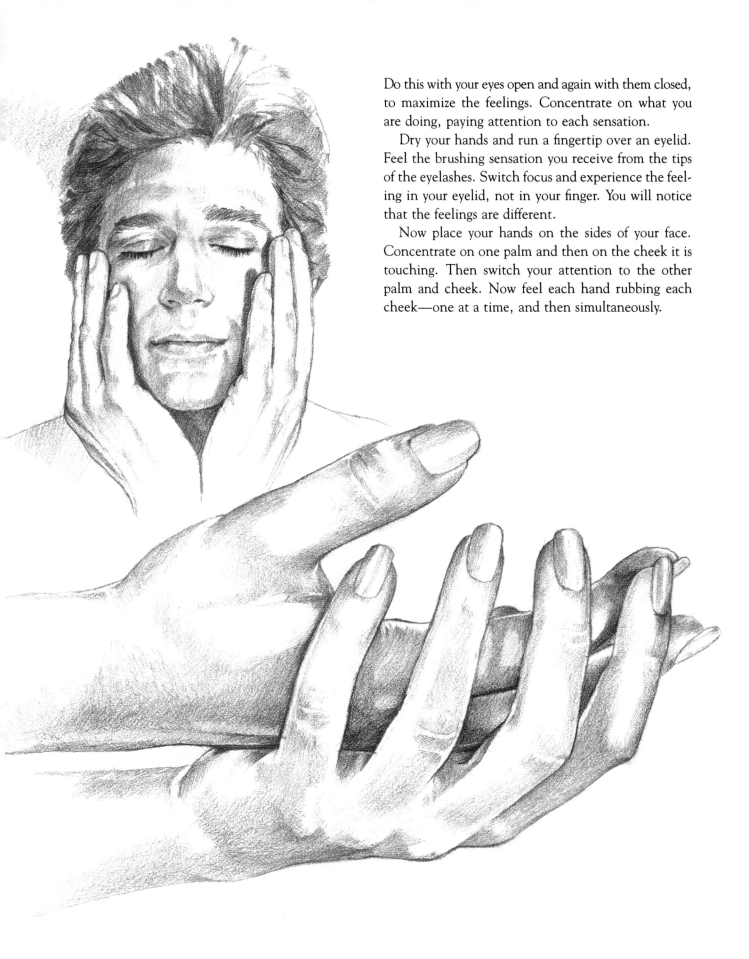

Do this with your eyes open and again with them closed, to maximize the feelings. Concentrate on what you are doing, paying attention to each sensation.

Dry your hands and run a fingertip over an eyelid. Feel the brushing sensation you receive from the tips of the eyelashes. Switch focus and experience the feeling in your eyelid, not in your finger. You will notice that the feelings are different.

Now place your hands on the sides of your face. Concentrate on one palm and then on the cheek it is touching. Then switch your attention to the other palm and cheek. Now feel each hand rubbing each cheek—one at a time, and then simultaneously.

As another way of learning about your feelings, here is an exercise called *the hand game*. It helps you take control and assume responsibility for your own pleasure, without depending upon another person to give your pleasure to you.

Place the back of your right hand in your cupped left hand so that a physical connection is made. Both hands are now one entity. Close your eyes.

Pretend that your left hand belongs to a partner.

Focus on the right hand, imagining that something is on the back of it. Concentrate on the feeling.

Now, keeping both hands quiet, switch focus to the palm of your left hand. What does that feel like?

Move the palm of the left hand along the back of your stationary right hand. Do this slowly and lightly, feeling the knuckles and little valleys between. Proceed gently, feeling what is going on in the back of your right hand. Continue by switching the feeling to the palm of the left hand as you continue moving it. Now stop the movement and just concentrate on the sensations in the palm of your left hand. Switch to the back of the right hand and see how that feels. Perhaps it will be a little tingly.

Now, separate the two hands very slowly so that you can barely tell when you are no longer touching. Concentrate on sending heat between the back of one hand and the palm of the other. Continue to separate your hands very slowly until you feel a blast of cold air, a signal that the connection has been broken and that your hands are now separate. Then perform the same exercise with the palm of your right hand and back of your left hand, keeping your eyes closed.

"I was home alone practicing the hand caress when I suddenly had the desire to test it out. My dog was curled up comfortably near me, and I decided to try the exercise with him. I stroked his body gently, noticing where he felt hard or soft. As I slowly outlined his musculature and bone structure with my palm he became very content and passive. Knowing that his most responsive part is his stomach, I gently stroked him there, watching all four paws extend upward, completely relaxed.

"Animals don't seem to need lessons in accepting pleasure. His response was honest and self-serving. He showed

no interest in my pleasure, and he made no attempt to reciprocate. I truly enjoyed feeling the silkiness and softness of his fur, while he simply took his pleasure as it was given."

This is what you want to develop—the ability to accept pleasure in the same, unselfconscious way. In an intimate situation, if you concern yourself with such things as whether or not your partner likes how you feel, the way you say things, or the way your body looks, it takes away from immediate feelings and replaces them with goals and anxiety. What you want is simply to remain focused on the moment.

Think about trying to appreciate the bouquet and subtleties of a glass of wine by gulping it down. Aside from a flash impression, you get little information about whether it was dry, full-bodied, or fruity. To enjoy the wine, you need to take just a sip, swishing it around your mouth and holding it there for a few seconds. The slower you go, the greater the flavor. A larger area inside the mouth is affected, and the pleasure is fuller and longer lasting.

When you acknowledge sensitivities, a connection will be made between you and your partner, regardless of the conditions.

"My lover had arrived at my house one evening to take me out to dinner and a film. We sat down in the living room to discuss which restaurant to go to. As we were talking, he was running his fingers gently over my knuckles, and I was looking through a magazine for dining suggestions. Before I knew it, without any warning, I had an orgasm. It was a tiny, rippling kind, but an orgasm nonetheless.

"We were both surprised, as there was nothing outwardly conducive to it. Although our conversation or nuances had in no way been sexual, we were connected; and since I had allowed that connection to flow freely, my body responded long before sexual thoughts ever reached my consciousness. It was at that point that I knew that the possibilities of stimulation and response are infinite."

The hand caress is the first and single most important step in this program. Once you understand the concept of touch as you have experienced it through your hands, you will be able to apply it to all of the steps in the chapters that follow.

FACE CARESS

It is fascinating to speak with plastic surgeons about the variety of cosmetic surgeries available today. Anyone with the desire to improve upon a certain feature and the money to cover the exorbitant cost can have a more defined chin, a smaller nose, flatter ears, droopless eyes, and a line-free face.

Moreover, being beautiful has become so high on people's priority lists that there is sometimes a long wait to get to see a doctor for consultation, and an even longer wait to get into the operating room. Although the cost of cosmetic procedures can run well into the thousands, people are flocking to have prettier faces.

Plastic surgery is somewhat extreme as a method of looking better, and it is certainly not in everyone's budget. Fortunately, there are less expensive ways to enhance one's face.

Facialists provide a viable service for retaining a healthy and perky-looking face, and in some cases they claim to help avert further lines and sagging. In addition to this benefit, the facial massage helps circulate the blood, which keeps the skin surface alive.

Professional facials cost upward of $35, and often the facialist recommends creams and lotions, which are available to the client at an additional cost. While facial salons once catered strictly to women, men can now be found resting comfortably while having their faces steamed and packed in a beauty mask.

Improving oneself is certainly worthwhile, but it is important to think carefully before deciding which route would best serve a particular need. While addressing

3

An exercise in taking the risk of asking permission to look and touch

possible solutions to the question of aesthetics, it is important to consider this aspect: Though aging and heredity play an enormous part in how one's face looks, stress also manages to surface through the pores and leave its mark on the prettiest and youngest of faces.

There are ways to take care of the face that do not require professional intervention or the expenditure of money. Everyone has a responsibility for making a personal effort toward creating a more peaceful and appealing face. One way to achieve this is through caressing one's own skin. Think about the high cost and possible medical risks of more extreme procedures. Then investigate the second step in your touching process—the face caress.

As before, prepare a comfortable and quiet setting for your touching experience. Use no lotions or oils in this exercise, as it is not necessary to prepare the face in any particular way. An unshaven or unblemished face is not an issue. In fact, facial hair and a variety of other textures add interest to the exploration.

Let us again assume that you are taking the active role first. Sit with your back supported by a wall or pillow, and have your passive partner lie on his back with his head resting on a pillow in your lap. As he allows the serenity and luxury of the situation to envelop him, he will close his eyes and sink into relaxation and concentration. You, however, will keep your eyes open, at least until you are thoroughly familiar with his facial structure. In gaining your partner's trust, the last thing you want to do is poke his eyes or catch the

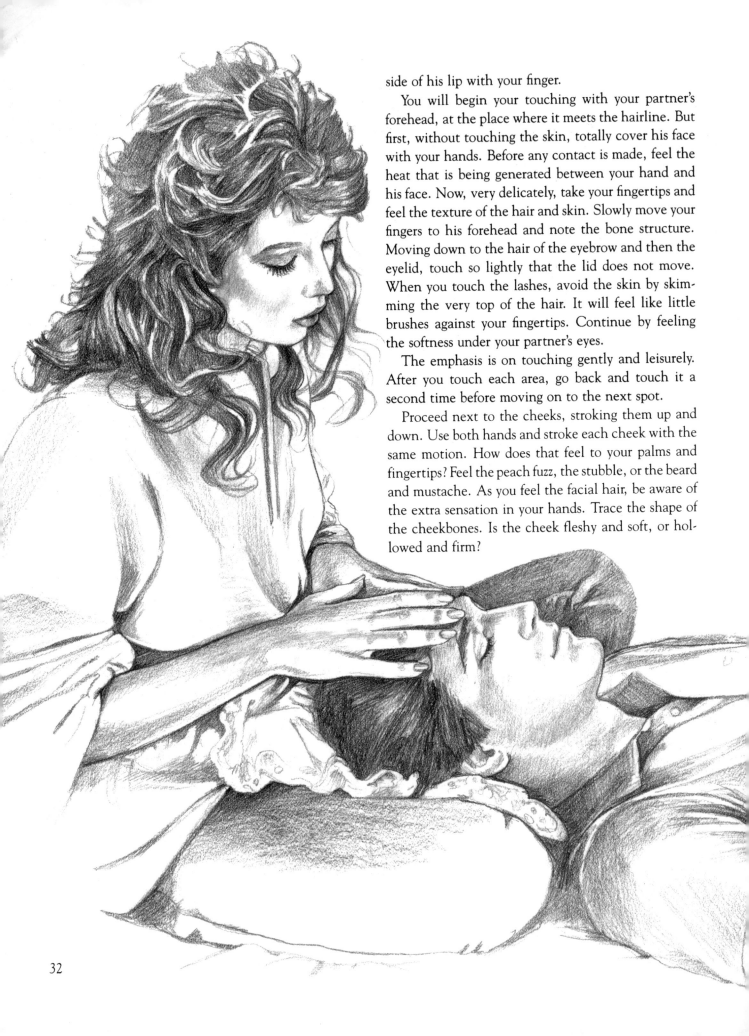

side of his lip with your finger.

You will begin your touching with your partner's forehead, at the place where it meets the hairline. But first, without touching the skin, totally cover his face with your hands. Before any contact is made, feel the heat that is being generated between your hand and his face. Now, very delicately, take your fingertips and feel the texture of the hair and skin. Slowly move your fingers to his forehead and note the bone structure. Moving down to the hair of the eyebrow and then the eyelid, touch so lightly that the lid does not move. When you touch the lashes, avoid the skin by skimming the very top of the hair. It will feel like little brushes against your fingertips. Continue by feeling the softness under your partner's eyes.

The emphasis is on touching gently and leisurely. After you touch each area, go back and touch it a second time before moving on to the next spot.

Proceed next to the cheeks, stroking them up and down. Use both hands and stroke each cheek with the same motion. How does that feel to your palms and fingertips? Feel the peach fuzz, the stubble, or the beard and mustache. As you feel the facial hair, be aware of the extra sensation in your hands. Trace the shape of the cheekbones. Is the cheek fleshy and soft, or hollowed and firm?

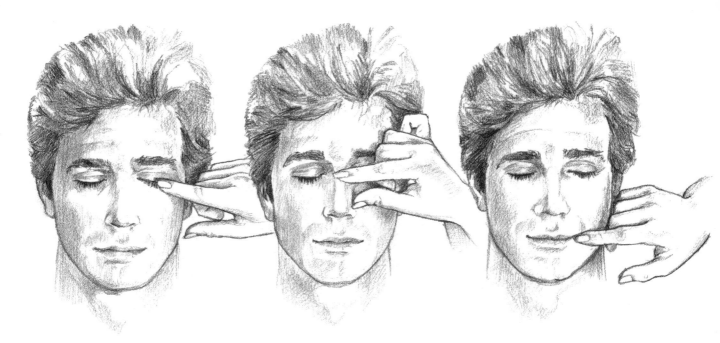

During this time your partner remains silent, his entire focus on his own face. He offers nothing in the way of feedback or assistance. He cannot observe what you are doing. He can only feel. As with the librarians in the research study, your touch is subtle and non-threatening. You are touching for yourself and your own pleasure. Your focus is on your hands and fingertips.

Using a thumb and index finger, outline your partner's jawbone. You can use both hands at once, or each hand separately. Run your index fingers down the sides of the nose, outlining the nostrils where they meet the cheek. Stroke the length of the nose to the tip, under it, and around the opening of the nostrils. You will want to be careful not to close off the nostrils with your fingertips.

Caress above the upper lip, feeling the mustache growth, and then proceed to the lips themselves. Very slowly, outline the edges and go into the corners. Caress

FACE CARESS

the flat of the lips. However, do not touch inside the mouth, even though there is a tendency for the lips to part while being stroked. This is a natural reflex, similar to that of an infant who, when her cheek or lips are touched, opens her mouth and begins feeding. It is instinctive behavior.

As you touch the chin, be aware of its shape. Is it pointed? Does it have a cleft? There are endless details to pay attention to if you take the time to notice. Taking the time to caress slowly and gently enhances the experience for both partners. The millions of sensory receptors on the skin's surface indicate to your partner how you feel about him; eventually, they help him to know better how he feels about himself.

When you begin caressing the ears, remember that you do not want to probe deeply inside. This might seem threatening and could also cause injury. There are many other parts of the ear that respond very successfully to touch, such as the front, the outer edge, the back, and the areas where the ear meets the skull.

Wherever there is a natural fold of skin, the nerve endings are bunched close to the surface. The folded skin protects them, because these areas are very sensitive. Carefully investigate all the folds in the ear, and move gently into all the surface convolutions. Feel the thickness of the lobe between your fingertips.

From the ears, move to the neck and collarbone.

In order to reach the back of the neck, it is necessary to gently lift your partner's head off the pillow with both hands, turn it to one side, and rest it on your palm. From this position you can caress the back of the neck on one side. When enough time has been spent there, turn the head again so that it now rests on the other palm. Repeat the caress on the other side of the neck. With your partner's head centered in your lap, stroke his hair, running your fingers gently through it. The scalp will receive messages through the hair at the same time and be pleasantly stimulated.

In the smaller sections of the face, caress with just the fingertips; on the larger spaces, use your whole hand. Each face has a definition of its own. By touching with interest, you are discovering its unique qualities. Remember to repeat each caress before leaving any particular area. This gives your partner maximum pleasure, since his face becomes more alive as the skin is sensitized. At the end of the caressing, cup your hands over your partner's eyes, hold them there for a minute, and then release.

Now is the time for both of you to express what you felt during the caressing. Be very clear in your choice of words, so that the conversation will be both instructive and constructive. Afterward, switch roles so that you will become the passive partner. At the end of the touching, again discuss your mutual feelings about the experience. The exercise should take about an hour.

"My seven-year-old daughter had a friend over one day, and they were outside in the yard playing a game. It first appeared to be Simple Simon, but then I saw that it was a variation on that theme.

"I was curious about their activity, so I walked outside to watch. They were in close proximity, maybe a foot apart, facing each other and sitting cross-legged on the grass. They took turns asking questions. It went something like this:

"'Please look at my nose.'
"The other child did so.
"'Thank you very much.'
"A few other parts of the face were looked at, and then it switched to, 'Please touch my ear.'
"Her request was fulfilled, and the child touching her was again thanked. Then they switched roles so that each child had a chance to be looked at and touched. Returning to the original order, the first child now asked,

FACE CARESS   35

'May I look at your eyes?'

"Upon agreement from her playmate, she said, 'Thank you very much.'

"Next, she asked if she might touch her friend's hair. She did and thanked her once again. I was absolutely fascinated by this process and asked them where they learned the game. They explained that it was something they played in school with their classmates, under their teacher's supervision.

"Very impressed, I visited the teacher one day and asked her more about the game. She explained it this way:

"'When the children reach a certain age they become more aware of differences among themselves. Some children are taller and more developed than others, and others are lighter skinned. A few of my students wear glasses, and some have six teeth missing, all in front. There is a tendency to ridicule, as children feel uncom-

How much is to be learned from child's play! If you and your partner play this same game of asking permission to look and touch, you each begin seeing the other as a person, rather than only as a member of another gender. This erases many obstacles. It helps you enter into each other's presence and makes it difficult to keep each other out.

This is an exercise in taking a risk, the risk of asking permission to look and touch, and possibly being refused. How does it feel when you are not granted permission to stare into your partner's big brown eyes? What is your response when your partner is unwilling to stroke your hair? Perhaps you are very disappointed. But if you do not ask for what you want, you have already said "no" to yourself.

How would you know the feeling of having your face stroked or your hand touched, unless you are willing to ask for it? Assuming that your partner is a mind reader seldom works.

If you are following this touch program by yourself, or if you would like to do some pleasant homework, the face caress is a relaxing and satisfying exercise to perform alone. You may either sit comfortably or lie down, allowing yourself perhaps half an hour of exploration of your skin, hair, and features. Touch slowly and attentively, and you will have a totally new experience of yourself. Go gently over and around each of your features, just as if you were exploring a partner's face. As you do this caress, remember that your comfort is an important part of the exercise.

The face caress allows all of the components of the face to be explored. You can now appreciate your own or your partner's face more fully—not only as a whole, but for all its many intricate and lovely parts. There is no such thing as just another pretty face; none feels the same as any other.

When you are the active partner in these touching exercises, we have encouraged you to remain totally focused on your own pleasure. As the passive partner, you have had the enjoyment of sitting or lying down, totally physically relaxed, while you focus on the touching. Let your body float with the sensations without analyzing them. Giving in to the floating feeling

fortable with the differences. The game is a way of breaking through the barriers they have created for themselves. It causes them to notice sameness, rather than difference.'

"I walked away feeling grateful that my child was being educated to something that had taken me many more years to learn."

is difficult for some people. It might be that the person is preparing to fall asleep, trying to sneeze, or on the verge of orgasm. If she does not let go and relax, she cannot achieve these functions. A desire to stay in control is often the reason that people hold back from orgasm. They sometimes fear they will float away, never to return. Saying "yes" to yourself and trusting the feeling will afford you greater pleasure and eliminate apprehension about having new physical experiences. With a little practice, you can learn to give up control and let the surrender become automatic.

Here is a breathing exercise that will clear your mind and help you to relax. Before you begin it stretch out on a bed or soft carpet and let your body go. Lift your shoulders high, toward your ears, tensing them as hard as you can. Then, very slowly, pull your shoulders down as far as you can, as though someone were pulling on your hands. You have exaggerated the tension, so there should be no resistance to letting go. Look at where your shoulders are now, and leave them there. This simple procedure helps bring about the process by which you can surrender to whatever you are going to be doing next.

With closed eyes, begin to breathe slowly and easily. Be aware of the air going in and out. Breathe in through your nose and out through your mouth. You are learning the basics of surrender.

Now make believe you have the stem of a balloon inside your diaphragm. Slowly breathe down the stem all the way to your diaphragm. Go past the lungs. Imagine filling the balloon with air, and then breathe out again, letting the air out of the balloon through your mouth. As you breathe, your stomach is rising and falling—swelling with air and then emptying again. Slow it down as much as possible and exaggerate your

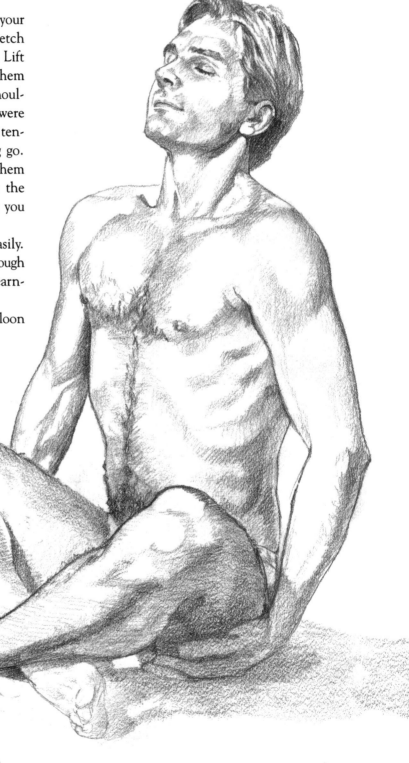

movements, until you can feel what is going on in the diaphragm area.

Next, try breathing in to the count of one and breathing out to the count of two. Play with it at your own pace. After practicing that for a bit, change it slightly: On the count of one, breathe in. When there is no more room to inhale, move into the second count,

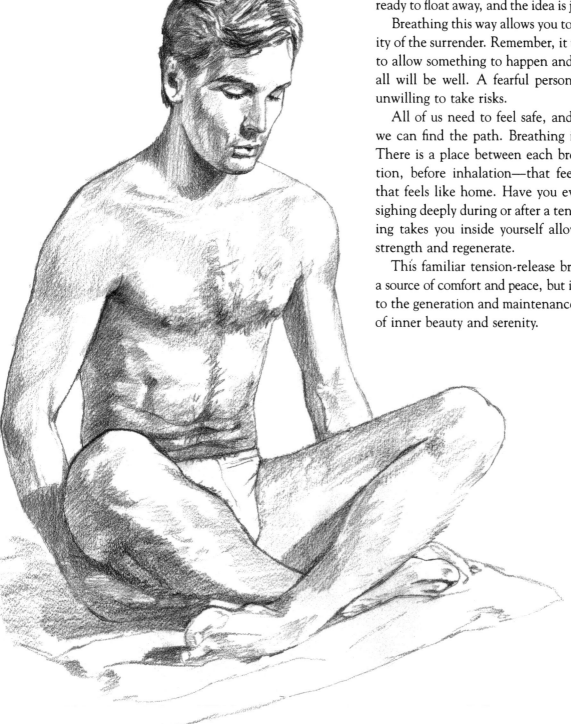

leaving everything wide open as though you had room to draw in more air. Do not tighten or hold your breath, but try floating into it until your body tells you it has had enough. On the three count, exhale. Down at the end of the breath, at number four, make believe you still have more air to release. Then be still, and wait for your body to tell you when to breathe in again.

What you are doing is breathing in easily, with no tension. The two and four counts are the important ones. That is where you wait for your body to tell you what to do next. You may also feel like you are getting ready to float away, and the idea is just to let it happen.

Breathing this way allows you to maximize the quality of the surrender. Remember, it takes inner strength to allow something to happen and feel confident that all will be well. A fearful person holds back and is unwilling to take risks.

All of us need to feel safe, and through breathing we can find the path. Breathing is like going home. There is a place between each breath—after exhalation, before inhalation—that feels safe and secure, that feels like home. Have you ever noticed yourself sighing deeply during or after a tense situation? Exhaling takes you inside yourself allowing you to gather strength and regenerate.

This familiar tension-release breathing is not only a source of comfort and peace, but is a natural approach to the generation and maintenance of a face reflective of inner beauty and serenity.

FOOT CARESS

4

The foot thinks the whole world is made of leather

The foot is perhaps one of the most overlooked parts of our anatomy, as well as one of the most fascinating. We stand on our feet for hours at a time, ignoring the fact that they are continuously working to support our entire body weight— not an easy job. When we relinquished the posture of being on all fours, we placed an extra burden on the feet, and they have had to endure the consequences. Crammed into trendy, uncomfortable shoes, they go through life thinking that the whole world is made of leather.

There is historical evidence, however, that the foot has been recognized in certain cultures as being a sensual and sexual part of the human form, a member worth revering.

In ancient China, despite attempts to outlaw the custom, footbinding was practiced for thousands of years. The "lotus foot," as it was called, was considered highly erotic and potentially useful in the art of making love. It is interesting to note that most Westerners have been under the illusion that footbinding was merely a method of keeping a woman's foot small and feminine, in addition to forcing her to step with a rather dainty, fragile gait. Other theories were that men bound their women's feet so that they could not run or move quickly, therefore rendering them incapable of escaping undesirable advances made by the opposite sex.

The lotus foot became an obsession of the Chinese male and was the object of sexual worship. A man would respond wildly when stroked by this misshapen, deformed, and mysterious extremity. He would become equally as excited when he caressed and kissed it and rubbed his genitals against it.

While it is doubtful that footbinding would gain any popularity today, the foot remains a very sensual part of our body, worthy of respect and acknowledgment.

As you begin the third phase of touching, the foot caress, be aware of the many possibilities available to you through the foot, and pay careful attention to your responses—old and new.

Prepare a bucket or small tub with warm, softened water. When you add a few drops of fragrant softener, the water texture enhances the caress and seduces the feet. You will each need two bath towels, soap, oil, lotion or powder. Make certain that all the supplies you need are ready before you begin, so there is no interruption during the caress.

As the active partner, gently take your partner's foot and set it into the tub of water. With the soap, very slowly wash the foot, and then leave it sitting in the water while you repeat the same steps with the other foot. Returning to the first foot, carefully lift it from the water and place it on your thigh, which is covered with a towel. Repeat the soaping routine and then return the foot to the tub while you do the other foot. After both feet have been amply lathered and rinsed, remove them from the water and place them in the towels, creating a baby bunting kind of wrapping around each foot. Then push the pan away from the area in which you are sitting, so that you have full clearance— an unencumbered environment in which to explore.

Gently unwrap the bunting from one foot and begin to dry it. Use the towel carefully in between the toes

FOOT CARESS

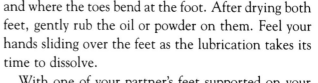

and where the toes bend at the foot. After drying both feet, gently rub the oil or powder on them. Feel your hands sliding over the feet as the lubrication takes its time to dissolve.

With one of your partner's feet supported on your thigh, begin stroking the top part, moving gradually to the ankle. Do this foot caress in the same manner that you did the hand caress. Let your fingertips and hands just barely glide along the outer and inner contour of the foot. If your partner indicates he is ticklish in some area, try to find a manner of touching there— probably a slightly firmer touch—that does not tickle. When it no longer tickles, resume lighter touching. On the sole of the foot, experiment with your fingers in combinations of two, three, and four, stroking the arch and sliding in between the toes. Then cup the heel with the entire hand. Roll each toe between your thumb and forefinger, very lightly, and with the same two fingers stroke them up and down.

After ten or fifteen minutes of caressing, do the same gentle exploration of the other foot. Then talk about your mutual experience before switching roles. You will need a fresh supply of water for the second half of the exercise. After your turn as the passive partner, once again express feelings about the exercise.

If either you or your partner is ticklish, the feet are usually the vulnerable spot. This is because there are so many nerve endings in the soles of the feet which are not used to being touched. This also means that your feet have enormous potential for sensual pleasure. It is not uncommon for a person to hold onto ticklish tendencies in the feet as a way of blocking feelings that may become sexual. As long as a person remains ticklish, he can avoid being touched. Try to get past any ticklishness. Let your feet enjoy the luxury of being stroked and pleasured by whatever surface they encounter.

When you are by yourself, you can further sensitize your feet by walking around barefoot on as many different surfaces as you can find: Walk in the kitchen and feel the tile and its smoothness underfoot. Walk through the grass in early morning when it is still covered with dew. Let your feet sink into the plush carpet

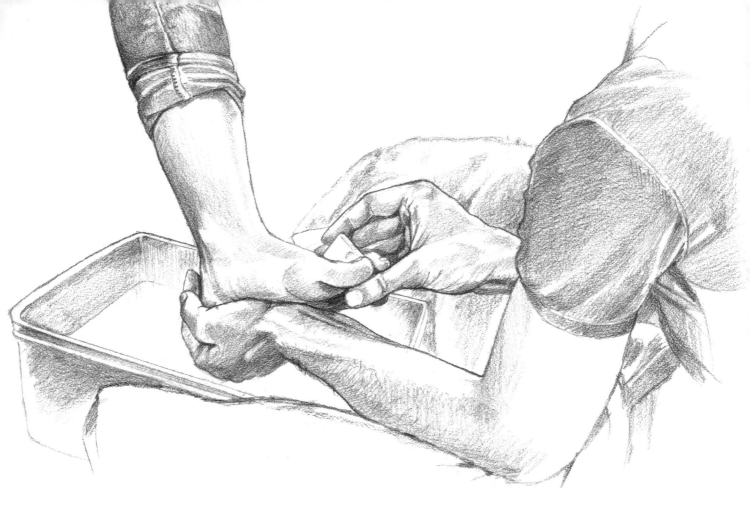

in the living room, feeling the bounciness under your soles. Stroll through the garden where the sun has warmed the ground, feeling your connection with the earth. Plant the soles of your feet on concrete or terrycloth and notice the rough texture. Place silk or satin on the floor and let your feet glide over its softness. Investigate as many surfaces as you can, noting your preference and response. Do you prefer the wet or the dry, the smooth or the rough, the warm or the cool? Being familiar with your personal preferences helps you to understand your sensual nature.

As you begin to experience new textures, you will also have an increased perception of your foot: its size, shape, and surface. Although aesthetics is not a major concern in the touching process, it is still important to keep your feet groomed and sensually appealing. Moisturizing lotion combats dry, scaly skin. Hot water soaks relieve fatigue and cramping. If you notice cal-

loused areas, have them removed; callouses tend to deprive the skin of sensation and the foot will be less responsive to touch.

You will want to do everything possible to keep your feet free from constraints of any kind so that when the opportunity arises for them to be pleasured, you can sit back and enjoy it.

"I was celebrating my birthday a few years back, and I had invited some close friends to my favorite restaurant to help me bring in my new year. We were laughing and eating and drinking champagne, being rowdy and doing justice to the occasion. Turning to a woman friend, I noticed an unusual kind of stare on her face, and I immediately became concerned. Trying not to be obvious, I remained silent and just studied her for a minute. Within seconds of my tuning in to her, she closed her eyes and her head tilted back; a beautiful smile covered her face and a blissful serenity enveloped her.

"Not wanting to disturb my friend's tranquility, I

resumed eating, but accidentally dropped my napkin from my lap. Diving under the table to recover it, I became amused at what I discovered. My mesmerized friend, who had caused me such concern, was not troubled at all. In fact, based on what I saw, the situation was quite the opposite. My good old bachelor buddy friend, who was sitting opposite her, had removed her socks and shoes and had propped her feet in his lap. The expression on her face became clearer to me as I saw his hand sensually caressing her feet and stroking her ankles. Politely, I grabbed my napkin and returned to an upright position, secretly wishing it was me instead of her."

This story is a reminder that the foot is an erotic organ with its own sexual nerves. It is one of the most sensitive tactile organs, capable of very intimate sensation. Like the hands, the feet can be used to caress your partner during lovemaking, giving you an additional two "hands" with which to stimulate. Each toe is loaded with sensuality, which in no small way supports the growing numbers of people who derive tremendous pleasure from having their toes kissed, sucked, and gently stroked.

When you are making love, notice how the toes may curl at times. This is because sexual tension sometimes begins in the foot, and if you are paying attention you will be aware of the tightening from the toes to the ankle. The nice thing about the foot is its easy access. You can practice the caress on your own feet, giving yourself pleasure while learning what feels good.

Take your time with the feet. They are a storehouse of untapped sexuality.

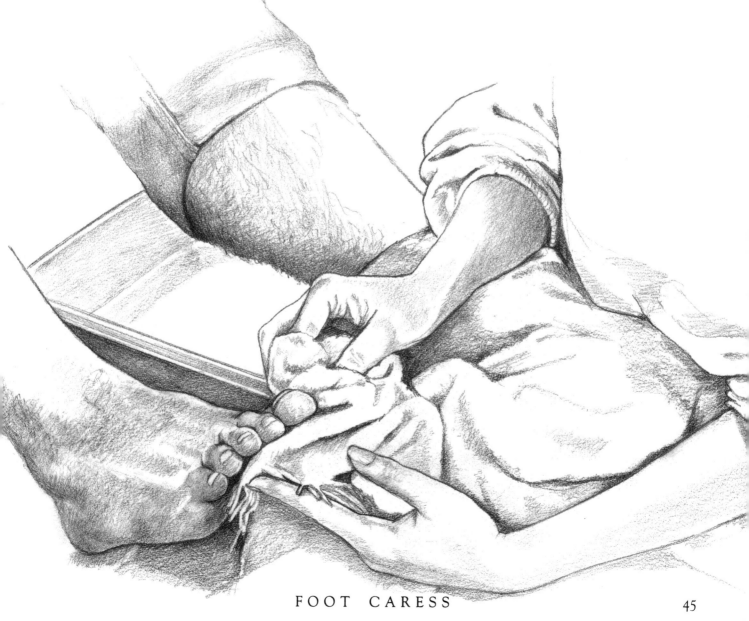

FOOT CARESS

BODY IMAGE

5

An "undress rehearsal" to give you a head start on becoming comfortable in the nude

"In 1974 I was invited to make a guest appearance on The Dinah Shore Show. *This was to be a golden opportunity for millions of viewers to be introduced to, and learn more about, surrogate work. I was very careful to dress in a tailored suit and blouse; I hoped I would be viewed as just another PTA-going mother, not as someone in an unusual profession. It worked, because when I came on stage the audience generated a kind of surprised and nervous laughter, apparently unprepared for the respectable image they saw before them.*

"As the interview began and Ms. Shore addressed the first question to me, I became very preoccupied with where the camera lens was, and at which angle they were shooting. All I could think was, 'Oh, no, the camera's got my nose!' Suddenly I was so involved in thinking about my looks that I wasn't present; I barely heard her question. I was consumed with concern over exposing my bumpy profile to all those television viewers. Then I remembered that there were twenty million viewers out there listening for my words, and I had lost sight of what was important. After what seemed like an interminable length of time (probably a split second), I regained composure and began to respond to the first question. To this day I have no idea what the question was, but I answered it and sailed through the rest of the show, maintaining my integrity and authority.

"Reflecting on the experience later, I realized how self-conscious I was about my nose. If it was going to interfere with my concentration, then I needed either to accept it or fix it. I had it fixed."

Vanity can be inappropriate and a major distraction. It interferes with how you relate to people, and it often inhibits people as they become more intimate.

If a person does not like a part of her body, often she will avoid being touched there.

There probably isn't a woman around who at some time has not felt nervous about spending the night with her lover, for fear of how he would view her without her makeup. This kind of thinking really gets in the way. It sometimes sabotages golden opportunities.

Until now, all of the touching exercises have been done fully clothed. You are ready to begin a new phase. From this chapter forward, all the exercises are to be done in the nude.

The purpose of the body image exercise is to evaluate your body and appreciate its uniqueness. It is exciting and educational to rediscover another part of who you are and to explore the values you place on your various body parts. Additionally, in this exercise you and your partner are breaking down barriers by revealing your bodies to one another. This ultimately relieves anxiety and creates more intimacy. You may make discoveries about yourself and your partner that will amaze you. No matter how long you have been living with your body or have been exposed to someone else's, there are endless things to learn from the body image exercise.

This time you and your partner begin by each working alone before doing any work together. If you are following the touch program without a partner, this is the only part of the exercise you can study until the time when you can do it with someone.

Your task is to become familiar with your own body image. Begin by standing nude in front of a full-length mirror. You may feel awkward with your nakedness at first, but that will pass in time. This is an "undress rehearsal," to give you a head start on becoming comfortable in the nude and being honest about what you see in the mirror.

Spend about a half hour looking at your reflection objectively, as though it belonged to someone else who has given you permission to stare. Evaluate this image from top to bottom, discussing aloud every angle, curve, and texture. Look deep into your own eyes. Pay attention to what you hear your voice saying. Be totally honest. Do not be thrown off course if you suddenly see a new freckle, or you notice that one shoulder is lower than the other. When you look carefully, every blemish, wrinkle, and dimple begins to surface, as does the loveliness of satiny skin and shapely legs. This is a re-education process; a wonderful opportunity to see your assets clearly, and perhaps to make decisions to accept or improve what you see.

Some of what you might complain about can be remedied. Dry-looking hair can be conditioned more often; cellulite-covered thighs can ride a bicycle; excess body hair can be permanently removed. Do the old pregnancy stretch marks plague you? Does the gash down your chest from your open heart surgery embarrass you? How can you accept the fact that once upon a time you were lean and firm, and now you are flabby and chubby? Try thinking of it this way: As you go through life, you accumulate markings, and they all tell a story of where you have been. How would it look, at sixty years of age, to have the body of a teenager? You may want that, but it does not match the road you have traveled. If you are now twenty pounds more in weight than when you finished high school, know that your body is showing twenty pounds more of living. Accept your passages gracefully and gratefully. Or if there is something you can do to improve yourself, do it and stop complaining about it. If your particular gripe is irreversible, then learn to love yourself unconditionally; see how much more beautifully you project yourself to others.

Next you are going to do the body image exercise with your partner. The first reaction to mutual nudity is different for everyone and also depends on the situation. But even with a partner of many years, disrobing in front of each other for the purpose of mutually looking and examining can feel awkward at first. There are a surprising number of couples who have been married for years and have never seen one another nude.

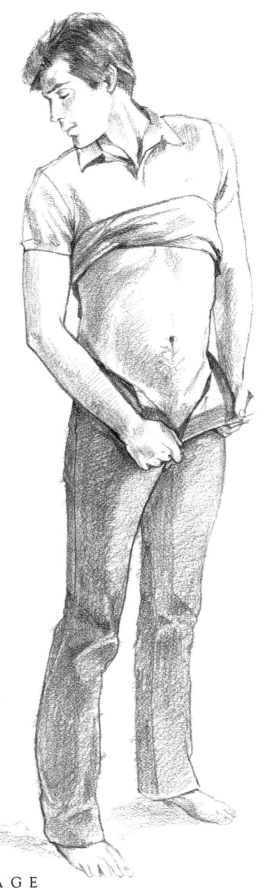

BODY IMAGE

"One of my clients told me that during his forty-year marriage his wife would always change her clothes in the bedroom closet, and they would make love in the dark. He never saw her nude. He went along with her modesty, always careful to cover up his own body. After their divorce he became my client, and he was still very uncomfortable about disrobing. At sixty-two, he first realized that by keeping their clothes on throughout their marriage, he and his wife had managed to avoid intimacy. As I started to remove my clothes for the first time, I noticed he was 'sneaking a peek' at me."

When you do the body image exercise, there is no need to sneak peeks. Permission is already granted. When two people consent to be naked with one another, they automatically allow their bodies to be observed. Remember, we are all naked under our clothes.

Keep in mind when you disrobe that your partner may be as self-conscious and nervous as you are. You may at first both feel like you're not sure where to look, now that you are standing naked in front of each other. Most people either peek at the breasts and genitals or avoid looking there entirely.

Some people initially have more trouble than others with being nude.

"There we were, sitting around stark naked, discussing how we would spend this session together. It was our third nude session, and he was still having a difficult time being naked. He was sneaking peeks, though I continually assured him that he could stare at me as much as he liked. On this particular day, he looked directly into my eyes and said, 'Gee, I never realized what blue eyes you have.'

"I felt we had won a major victory. He had noticed something other than my breasts and genitals."

Once you get used to being in the nude with each other, you no longer think about the nakedness. Your partner is not a nude body anymore, just a person.

The next part of this exercise will help put you both at ease. To begin, you and your partner stand nude, facing each other. You are going to find out at what distance apart you both feel comfortable. Stretch out your arms and touch each other's shoulders. You are now an arm's length apart. Talk about how that feels. Are you too close, not close enough? Do you feel threatened, lonely, crowded, disconnected? Through experimentation, discover the distance you both need

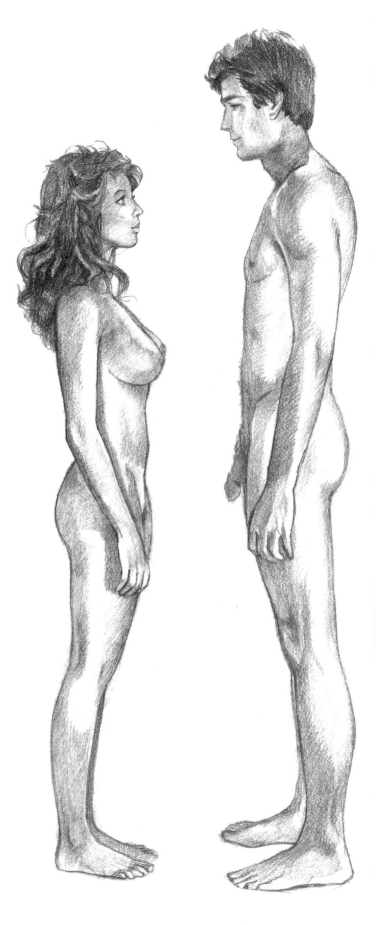

between you. This will vary among partners. A far-sighted person may back off, and his action will be misinterpreted as coldness. Another person may move in too close. An arm's length is often a good compromise, but it is up to each of you to determine what feels best.

Now that you have established spatial comfort, continue to face each other, still with hands on each other's shoulders, and close your eyes. Tune into your breathing pattern, and then connect with your partner's breathing. If one is breathing faster than the other, each gradually adapts to the other's rate, until you are both breathing in the same rhythm. Be very focused on your partner's breathing; let your chest cavity rise and fall as his does. This breathing together is a fun-

damental connection. In a situation such as lovemaking, it provides you with an intimacy that is unequaled. Once you are both breathing in harmony, you no longer pay attention to it; it becomes automatic.

When the breathing connection has relaxed you, drop your arms to your sides, but continue standing the same distance apart. Now begin to stare at each other candidly and guilelessly, like children do before they are told that staring is rude. Without talking, just look at the entire body very slowly. Start by looking at each other's hairline, and nothing else. You notice that the hair either curls or it does not; that it is brown, not blond. When you have fully explored that area, move to the forehead. Staring at the forehead is not easy, because there is an overwhelming desire to make eye contact. But stay with the forehead, and then move to the eyes. Stare into each other's eyes for a long time, until you feel comfortable.

Now look at your partner's nose, his cheeks, mouth, neck, shoulders, arms and hands. Move from area to area very gradually. Take a long, deliberate look at the breasts. Then proceed to the belly. Stare again when you reach the pubic area. The genitals and breasts are the two areas that attract us most and are most forbidden. Stare until you have had enough, or until it becomes just another part of the body. Eventually you will want to move on and have a good look at the next areas, the legs and feet.

Learn everything about this body: warts, moles, and all. Take turns staring at each other's backs. It does not matter whether you like what you see, or would prefer not to see it. Every scar, every vein, every pore on a person's body is what distinguishes that body from another. View this body with curiosity, not judgment. It just is. Judgment comes from imprinting. Allow your partner to discover all the wonderful things about you that make you uniquely who you are.

There is no conversation during this time, just observation. Spend about a half hour observing.

For the next part of the exercise, you and your partner will take turns at being passive and active, as in previous exercises. As the active partner, stand in front of the mirror and evaluate your body aloud—as you have already done when you were alone. Your partner sits quietly and watches you. You will probably need about forty-five minutes to thoroughly critique your body. An interesting part of doing the body image is that your response to yourself may vary each time you do it. Often your aesthetic perception of yourself is dependent on how you feel emotionally or physically. Sometimes we get dressed in the morning and feel like we need a complete body and face makeover, and even that might not do it. Yet there are other times when we glow at our reflection, and feel totally confident about ourselves.

Start at the top of your head, noticing your hair for its color and texture. Does it need a shaping or a rinse to perk it up? Then move down to the face and look at every feature separately, spending time on really seeing the thickness of your eyebrows and the shape of your eyes. Is your nose straight; are your lips full, or your cheekbones high? Does your chin jut out and is your jawbone very prominent? Talk out loud, honestly commenting on what you see in front of you, as though no one else were in the room.

Compliment yourself on your qualities that are pleasing to you. This may be difficult, since many of us have been taught to be self effacing, never conceited or narcissistic. Think of the body image exercise as an opportunity to praise your good points to your partner. You deserve to have them noticed and to enjoy them yourself.

"I was doing body image with a paraplegic client, who was observing me from his wheelchair. I focused on my thighs, bitching about how heavy they were, and as I ranted on, I caught a glimpse of him in the mirror. There sat a man, confined to a wheelchair, with a deformed leg that bent at the knee and was held up almost to his armpit. His body was spasmodic, his speech was unclear, and he was watching a perfectly healthy but ungrateful woman complain about her fat thighs.

"I turned around to him and said, 'I can't go on with this. It's ludicrous. Here you are, having never been able to walk, dependent on others for mobility, unable to enjoy physical functions that I take for granted. If I don't like my figure, I can get off my lazy butt and exercise. There's nothing you can do to change your situation.'

"He responded by urging me to continue doing the exercise, and because it was one of the prescribed steps

in the program, I had no choice but to proceed. I explored my body down to my toes, still being critical because that was honestly how I felt. Then it was his turn. He wheeled himself over to the mirror and carefully assessed his image.

"'I have very nice skin, and I like my hair and eyes very much.' He continued down every part of his body, and then talked about his leg that had been defective since birth. The bones had grown, but since he had no muscle tone, the leg had atrophied.

"'Someday you'll see. I'm going to straighten this leg out.'

"I have never felt so ashamed. This dear man taught me to accept myself and to use my energy on more positive issues than flabby thighs."

As you continue with the body image exercise, be aware of your neck and shoulder area, the length and shape of your arms and hands, your breasts, stomach, genitals, legs, and feet. If you want to touch any part of yourself as you are looking, do it.

When you look in the mirror, see the possibilities rather than the restrictions.

After you have covered all the territory, ask your partner to comment on what he saw and heard. You may be shocked or flattered. He may point out aspects of yourself that you have never noticed or not appreciated. What may seem like a fat body to you may be described as "voluptuous" by him. The pallor of your skin, which looks sickly bland to you, may be adored by your dark-skinned lover.

"In the middle of doing the body image exercise with a client, I began to feel anxious about exposing my rear view to him. He was in his prime at twenty-seven and had a gorgeous body with a very tight little butt. The panic that I felt was embarrassment at how much bigger and flabbier mine was, and I didn't want him to see me. But I maintained my role and continued. Then it was his turn. He stood in front of the mirror and said, 'I really hate my rear end. It's too narrow. I wish I had one more like yours, with a little more width and meat on it.'

"When we both completed the exercise, we talked about what he thought about his butt, and what I thought about my butt, and what we both thought about each other's, and soon we were laughing hilariously. The laughter broke the tension, and we were able to lighten up about what we thought was so negative a feature about ourselves. If this man had been a boyfriend instead

BODY IMAGE

of my client, and I had the opportunity of hiding, I might never have discovered that he liked my butt just the way it was."

When we go through life feeling inadequate and undeserving because we somehow feel inferior, we deny ourselves the possibility of a lot of pleasure.

After your partner has commented on his perception of your body, it is his turn to be the active partner. While he critiques his own body, you sit silently and observe, learning how he feels about himself. Afterward, you give him your responses.

In doing the body image exercise you learn much about yourself and your partner. Often it enlightens even long-term relationships. After 50 years of marriage a man may find out that his wife has never liked her breasts, which is why she actively discouraged him from touching them. A woman discovers that her man secretly wishes he had smoother skin, a hairier chest, or larger feet. Although she thought she knew her partner well, these secret desires had never surfaced. Generally, people conceal their feelings of inadequacy for fear they might reveal something that would turn their partner away. But the result of doing the body image together is that each of you no longer needs to hide your fears about who you really are. You and your partner now know each other from a new perspective. When you have both been willing to be vulnerable, and when you can say to one another, "I never knew you felt that way about that," your relationship is being strengthened and deepened. The rewards of the body image exercise can be immeasurable.

In doing this study, pay close attention to which areas your partner ignores as he critiques his body. Ask him to notice which areas of your body you ignore. It is not uncommon for a person to completely omit an area that he does not like or feels uncomfortable addressing. There are so many reasons why parts of the body become problematic to people. It takes just one bad experience to cause a person to become self-conscious about his anatomy. Being told that your genitals are the wrong size, that your breasts droop, that your bones stick out, or your feet are too big can change the way in which you communicate physically to others. We relate this way to each other all the time, and if

we accept the criticisms, then we have allowed a part of us to shut off, sometimes permanently.

A good homework exercise is to touch the areas that you omitted or criticized while doing your self-analysis. These ignored parts need more attention than the parts you more readily accept. As you gently attend each unloved part, ask yourself these questions: What does this part of me look like? What does it feel like? Does it function? There is nothing wrong with wanting to be well groomed and attractive, but the cosmetic factor is the least important consideration. Be cautious about putting emphasis on superficialities. Give respect to a healthy, sound, and functioning body.

So many of us are busy presenting a facade to the world. We feel a certain way inside but dress in a way that masks how we feel. We cover up our bodies, hiding our sensuality. Why not let yourself be discovered? Be aware of your best features and build on them; share them with others. The key to positive projection is to appreciate all of yourself.

"I had a friend who could walk into a room filled with people and draw every man to her side. I just didn't understand it. I'd spend hours primping for an evening out, and go completely unnoticed. It wasn't as if she was gorgeous, with a knockout body. She was overweight, had blemished skin and nondescript hair. We were close enough that I felt I could indulge my curiosity and find out her secret. So I asked her how it was that she was always surrounded by men. She responded by saying, 'If you've got it, flaunt it.'

"Well, from where I was sitting, she sure didn't have it. I pondered her answer for days, trying to understand how she could have thought she 'had it.' She looked awful at the time, struggling with diets, skin creams, and hairstyles. And then it dawned on me. What she was really saying was, 'whatever you've got, flaunt it.' The man with the deformed leg, my overweight friend, the aged, the wrinkled; whatever you have and wherever you are in life, flaunt it."

You will attract, as long as you hold positive thoughts about yourself. We lose and gain weight, our bodies change shape, our hair disappears or turns gray, our stamina lessens, but inside we remain beautiful to the very last. It is up to us to project that beauty outwardly.

Accept yourself, wrinkles and all; and *whatever* you've got, flaunt it.

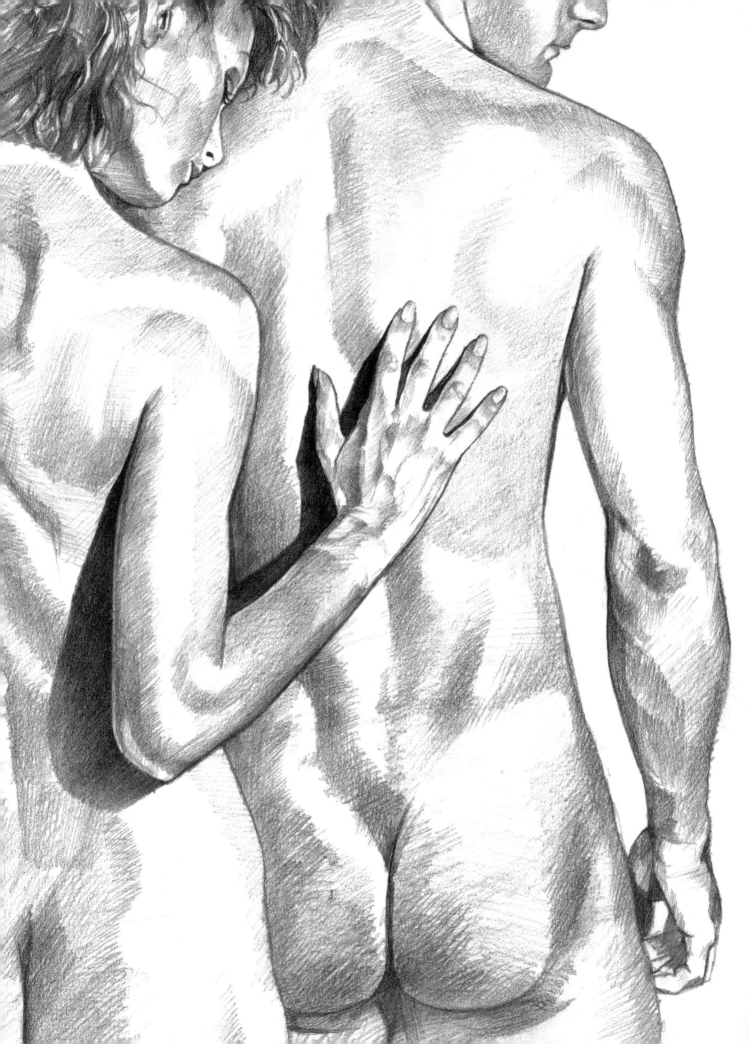

BACK CARESS

6

Now you have
a larger
playground
in which
to have fun and
get a bit
more creative

As you began your touching with the hand caress and then moved to the face and foot, you may have sensed that the pattern of movement was going from the extremities inward. The body image study introduced nudity, which ultimately brought you closer to physical intimacy.

The back caress gives you an opportunity to move freely over the body, without the constraints of small, defined areas. You now have a larger playground in which to have fun and get a bit more creative. Stretch out on a soft rug or bed and, as usual, make the environment as comfortable as possible. As you are both nude, make sure that if you choose the carpet you place a sheet or blanket beneath you. You may also want to lie on a towel or have one nearby if you are using oil for the caress. You have a choice of oil or powder, whichever appeals to you both. Allow a leisurely half hour for each of you to be in the active role.

During this caress you will both have your eyes closed so that nothing will distract from the tactile experience. As we mentioned earlier, there is a great deal of visual noise involved in the process of looking. The active partner will be sitting, kneeling, and straddling, but never exerting full body weight on top of his partner. Using a variety of positions eliminates tedium or cramping from being in one position too long. Comfort is essential, because the slightest physical disturbance distracts from what is taking place. The entire back of the body, from head to toe, is within limits for caressing; so take advantage

of all this new space. The passive partner is lying on his stomach, with a pillow under his head if desired; or a pillow can be placed underneath the hips to reduce pressure on the lower back. Make sure that your partner is comfortable. During the caress, if he is experiencing discomfort with your position, move slightly or switch to another part of his body.

As you begin this caressing as the active partner, you can be more imaginative than before. Now you can use more than your fingertips and hands. Think of all the possible ways in which you can touch your partner's back, using your wrists, inner arms, knees, feet, and even your whole body.

Both of you are silently taking your pleasure as you explore a wider range of touch possibilities. As the active person, let your partner know that your hand is present before you make your first landing. Since he cannot see where your hands are going to touch, it is comforting to have some clues. Soon you will both feel when the energy is right between you. Your partner will be concentrating on where he feels the caress and where you will be moving next, and *touch anticipation* begins. Maybe you will choose to move from the shoulder to the elbow. As you prepare to land on the skin, hold your hand over his shoulder, letting the heat generate to his skin. Gently place the hand down. Caress once from the shoulder to the elbow. Lift your hand off and tell your partner that you are going to caress him again in the same place. Ask him to anticipate where your hand will be as it moves across his skin, before he actually feels it. Since he is already focused on the upper arm and elbow, all of his feeling will be in the area and he will anticipate the movement of your hand there. You must not go off course or surprise him by going to another area. Repeat the caress several times, lifting off your hand in between, until your part-ner is able to anticipate the entire caress just ahead of your hand's touch.

After you finish your exploration in that area, tell your partner where next to anticipate you.

Practice touch anticipation with your partner on other areas of his body, to increase his sensitivity. The ability to be ahead of the touch creates heightened feelings of pleasure in the area being caressed. It becomes mesmerizing to the passive partner.

Also explore *touch memory* with your partner by telling him that you are going to move your hand from where it is, and he is to hold on to the memory of what he has just experienced. When your partner is sensitized to the energy between your hand and his skin, he can still feel the heat of your hand after you have lifted it from his skin. Practice touch memory as you caress various parts of his body, lifting your hand from the skin and asking him to remember the feeling there. To check out the progress of touch memory, lift your hand off your partner without telling him and see if he notices immediately. In a few seconds he may tell you that he no longer feels your touch, but he may not be quite sure how long it has been since you removed your hand. If his sensitivity is great, it can be as long as a minute, sometimes even longer, before he notices.

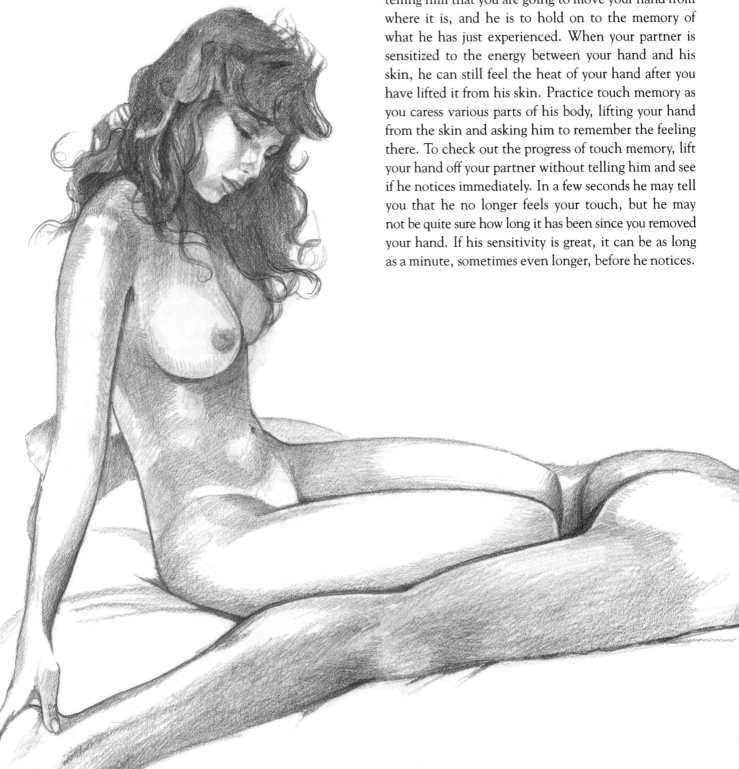

"We were about twenty minutes into the back caress, and my client had not stirred from the beginning. I watched goose bumps forming before I reached certain areas of his skin. His body was turning on in anticipation. I wasn't sure whether he was even awake. I leaned over and whispered in his ear, asking him if he was still there. He responded with a kind of positive humming sound, letting me know that not only was he there, but he was feeling good.

"I decided to test my theory of memory, so I gently removed my hands from his buttocks. After fifteen seconds or so, I asked him how it felt. He whispered that it felt exquisite, and to please continue doing more of the same. I repeated my question a few more times, until some minutes had elapsed. Even I was impressed at this man's concentration and sensitization. I resumed caressing him, and after I was through I asked him if he was aware of my touch at all times. He replied in the affirmative. When I told him of my experiment, he was incredulous. He still believed that I had never stopped touching him."

The back caress is very enchanting, and it is not uncommon for the person being caressed to simply float away. As always, the active partner is taking his goodies, enjoying the other person's body for himself. While the touching is taking place both partners are together in each particular moment. If the touching stops from time to time, the partner keeps the memory that allows his skin to hold on to the pleasure. That is the *afterglow*, the time for savoring all the wonderful feelings he has been experiencing.

The passive partner may fall asleep, and it is acceptable for him to surrender to it. The active partner is still touching, continuing to get what she needs from her partner's skin. It does not matter whether the person inside the skin is awake or asleep; the skin knows it is being touched. Falling asleep is also a barometer of the level of trust that has been established. The person does not feel compelled to stay awake to observe and control his situation. He flows with it.

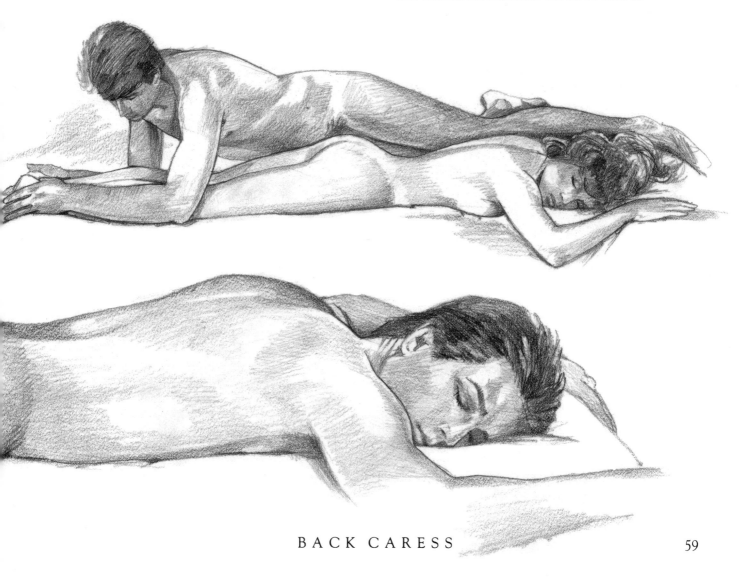

BACK CARESS

You will occasionally need to replenish the powder or oil you are using. There is a way of doing this so that your partner's back is never left unattended. Turn one palm up and gently keep caressing with the back of your hand, using the same slow movement. With the free hand, shake the oils or powder into the palm. Chances are your partner will not even notice. Or you can quietly replenish your supply while you are practicing touch memory.

If you want to caress with just one hand, leave the quiet hand at rest on the back somewhere. When both hands are being used, make sure you move symmetrically in the same area. Stroking his neck while caressing his thigh is very distracting, since he is forced to be aware of two areas at the same time. Explore the back from the neck to the toes. A variety of touching combinations is possible in this caress, and if you let yourself go with it, you will enjoy yourself tremendously. Let your foot glide down your partner's leg until your foot is connected with his. Slide your arm across his upper torso and shoulders. Fit your knee under the crevice of his buttocks and gently stroke that area. Allow your hair to drape across his body, quietly waking up the skin. Sweep your entire body over his, without applying any weight. Absolutely anything goes, providing there is no intentional genital contact or

talking during the caress—except for your very quiet instruction during the touch anticipation and touch memory practice.

Have you noticed how much more sensitized your hands have become since you first did the hand caress? Are you aware that you touch differently now than you did before? Gradually, as the process evolves, you feel the awakening of your sensuality.

Before you and your partner switch roles, and again after you have experienced both roles, give constructive feedback. Then do the entire exercise again, but this time with dialogue. (Any of the touching exercises can be done a second time, either with or without conversation.) The passive person is encouraged to

say, "lighten up," or "slow down," or "over there," and so on. Or he can take his partner's hand and show her what he would like. Remember, that at any time both of you have the right to say "no" for any reason. The right of refusal is central to the touching program.

It can be difficult to know how to instruct a partner without offending. How do you ask for something different without sounding like you are unhappy with what you are getting? Express your needs and wants lovingly, without guilt or fear. It is the responsibility of the listener to hear the words positively and to do whatever is needed to make the encounter a better one. It is unrealistic to assume we can know what a partner wants and likes at any given moment. Feedback eliminates misunderstanding and saves a lot of counterproductive time.

All of the exercises and caresses in this program share a common denominator. They are designed to generate vulnerability and closeness between two people. In this gradual process the partners begin to have a keener sense of the energy they are creating between them. The result of this heightened awareness is a sense of oneness that perpetuates a deeper warmth, sensitivity, and understanding.

Sometimes this oneness is easy to come by, and other times it takes a little work. But be assured that

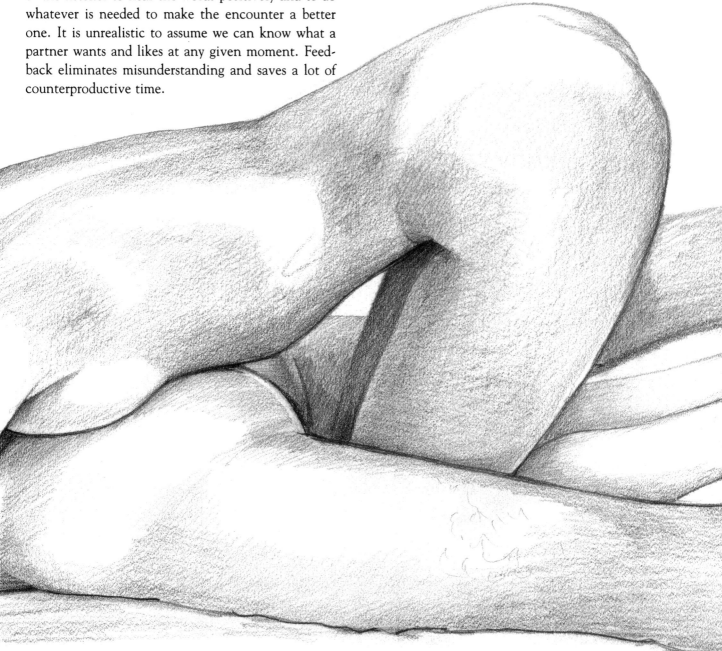

when you make the effort, it is worth the journey.

Spoon breathing is a rapid, effective way to achieve oneness with your partner, and it is relatively easy to do with each other. At the end of the back caress, the active partner's heart and breathing rates are much faster than the passive partner's. This is obviously because the person receiving the caress is relaxed and is not exerting any effort while the person giving the caress has been using a lot more energy.

Both of you now lie on your sides, the passive partner in front, with her back to her partner. The active person snuggles up to the back of his partner, creating a position much like two spoons fitting into each other. This is a comfortable and close position, and as you lie quietly next to one another, listen to both heartbeats. Then consciously make an attempt to merge with each other, ending up breathing together at the same depth and rhythm. The active person will have to slow his breathing down, while the passive one will start activating his breathing to where it becomes more rapid. This requires concentration at first, but as your quiet and meditative mood continues, you will both slow down, no longer aware of the process; and the breathing will become simultaneous. A sense of serenity surrounds you, and a feeling of intimacy has now been established. The spoon position is a loving way to fall asleep with your partner. Some couples are able to remain in that position and breathing pattern throughout the night, while others choose to separate after a while.

Take turns being in front and in back of your partner during the spoon breathing. Also, see if you feel different on your left side as opposed to your right. You may have a definite preference for a particular side, and it does not matter which you prefer, as long as you are both feeling pleasure as a result. Take inventory as you lie there, identifying where you are both touching each other. If you are in front, you may be aware of your partner's knee, breast, penis, stomach, ribcage, or pubic hair, but you will be deriving your pleasure from your shoulder blade, buttocks, arm, neck, or wherever it is you are being touched.

During the back caress, if you find yourself anxiously anticipating the genitals, then you have missed the point. There is more to a body than breasts or a penis. The neglected parts and imperfections need special attention. Stroking a scar, caressing the backs of the legs, or gently touching an abrasion is comforting to the person being touched. You are accepting all of him, not just the stereotypically appealing parts.

The entire body has appeal, and it is each partner's responsibility to discover it. Approach the back not as a flat, one-dimensional piece of skin. Explore the roundness of the shoulders and buttocks, and trace the hills and valleys of the skeleton and muscles from head to toe. Enjoy the thickness of the body, and all the folds and crevices.

The active partner is encouraged to move around for comfort and freedom. This movement also allows more opportunity for discovery. Straddle your partner

with your bent knees on the outside of his legs, then reach in between his thighs with your palms. Pay particular attention to the sides of the body. We have a tendency to touch the front or the back, neglecting the sides. If you recall, in the hand caress you were told to touch the outer and inner part of the hand and in between each finger. The outer and inner edges of the body are very sensitive, and it would be a great loss to ignore these areas. When you touch along the sides of the body, you will also feel the texture of whatever your partner is lying on, such as a silk sheet or a down comforter. In one movement, you are feeling both skin and fabric.

Even though you have been instructed not to intentionally touch the genitals, it is possible that you may brush a genital area because of its proximity to whatever else you are touching. Do not be alarmed if that happens. Unintentional brushing past the genitals is sometimes unavoidable. For example, if your male partner is lying on his stomach and you are caressing his buttocks, his testicles or a portion of his penis may be peeking through. When your partner is caressing inside your upper thigh, he may inadvertently stroke some pubic hair. Just remember that the genitals are not to be touched purposely at this time, no matter how much you may desire to do so. You are learning about taking time. There is no race to win or finish line to cross. The longer you take, the more you get.

The back caress is an extremely nurturing exercise and an exciting and sexy experience. You are the director and, within the rules, you create whatever scenario you choose. The back caress is anything but boring. Some lovers, even after years of being together, at times will choose a back caress over intercourse.

The biggest problem with long-lived relationships is that the partners tend to take each other for granted. They forget the days of courtship when they walked hand in hand along the beach or hugged tightly at the end of the day. You never need to lose that quality in your relationship, but it is not something that is maintained easily. It takes working at, and remembering all the simple pleasures you have shared. Long-standing relationships often mean an obligatory sex act before the lights go out at night, a habit without any real sensitivity to each other's deeper needs. A quick release is appropriate and even fun sometimes, but not when it becomes a steady diet. We get into ruts and frequently cannot find our way out. It is critical for you both to learn to experience the pleasure inherent in your entire body, not just during the exercises but as part of your everyday lives together. You must maintain this awareness for as long as the relationship exists. Otherwise the sensuality and the interest dwindle.

The quality of a relationship remains higher when one understands the difference between just having sex and making love.

FRONT CARESS

7

Performance pressures can often be inhibiting

A few chapters ago you learned about body image, and you were permitted to stare at your partner's body in a deliberate and obvious way. Doing this made all the body parts count, both in their importance and visual accessibility to you and your partner. We called special attention to the usually "sacred" parts; you raised your comfort level in being nude.

The front caress is done in two parts. In the first part, you are to touch your partner from head to toe, deliberately avoiding breasts and genitals. Allow twenty minutes for each of you to experience this. In the second part, after the completion of the nongenital caress, you move into a front caress in which you include the breasts and genital area, but only in a very casual way. With each step comes an assortment of attitudes and feelings that teach you even more about your body and its responses.

Avoiding the genitals while you caress your partner is likely to be a new experience. How does it feel to hold back your own desires, or your own demands? Performance pressure is often inhibiting. You can become so concerned with whether you are touching your partner in a way that is pleasing and stimulating to him that your anxiety blocks your tactile sensations.

When you are in the passive role, you will have the opportunity to feel what it is like not to be grabbed. Perhaps your breasts and genitals will feel lonely and unloved. It is more likely, however, that you will discover the intensity of feeling that comes from not being touched.

The front caress is based on a "touch-feel" premise: If you are touched everywhere except on the sexy places, how does that feel? Obviously your mind does not ignore the breasts and genitals, but when your body is caressed without stimulation to them, you allow a heightened response to develop. When a person does not feel the need to fight off premature advances, there is more willingness and desire to participate. Additionally, when the breasts and genitals are ignored, the body usually shows signs of wanting to be touched: a rippling of the skin, goose bumps, erect nipples or penis, or genital lubrication. The breasts and genitals lean forward and present themselves. The skin actually reaches out.

Choose oil or powder to do this caress, and make sure that you and your partner are as comfortable as you can be. The passive partner lies on his back and just receives his pleasure.

Beginning as the active partner, take your time moving down the body, using long strokes over the whole length and width. Be creative in your touching, as you were in the back caress. When you arrive at a breast, caress all around it, but not on the breast itself. The same goes for the genital area: Touching above and below is acceptable, but not any closer. At the end of the caress, you and your partner express your feelings about the experience, as usual.

Then switch and you take the passive role. Do you feel relief at not having to rush into the sex act just because your partner is touching your naked body, or do you find yourself getting excited and impatient to

FRONT CARESS

be touched everywhere? Whatever it is that you are feeling, accept it and flow with it, as there is much to be learned at this stage.

The front caress is an introduction to another phase of your sexual experience, which is *containment*. Containment is what you practice when you are highly excited but have no immediate outlet for that energy.

"A colleague of mine invited me to a lecture he was giving to sex therapists. Eager to hear more about what he was learning in the field of sexuality, I was happy to attend and had a front row seat. His talk, just by virtue of the subject matter, was highly stimulating as well as informative, and I could just feel the energy rise all around the room. There was a quiet buzz of sexuality throughout the audience, and it was apparent that he had reached his listeners on all levels. What struck me most was his command of his topic and his comfort with openly discussing the various issues he was addressing. He seemed charged with electricity, and I remember feeling that I had never seen him more brilliant.

"After the lecture, we went out for coffee and I commended him on the evening and how effectively he had handled his audience and material. He laughingly told me that it was not without discipline that he had gotten through the lecture and then proceeded to share his secret: 'Halfway through, I found myself so aroused by my own words that I had acquired a nice, big, fat erection. Fortunately the podium guarded my dilemma, while I let the erection work to my advantage. I poured all that sexual energy into my expression and presentation, and that's why you responded to me with such enthusiasm. I was turned on and projected that to my audience.'"

What this man was practicing was containment. He was using his sexual power in an appropriate and constructive way. He understood the value of being charged up, and he also understood that those feelings cannot always be channeled into sex. When you contain sexual energy until it is either appropriate or possible to do something about it, you hold on to the sensations. See where they take you. All your senses may be sharpened: Colors look brighter, flowers smell sweeter, and food tastes better while you remain in this state. You are allowing the natural flow of sexual response to move freely through your body.

At one time or another you may have practiced containment without realizing it.

"I was at a party with my husband and I found myself attracted to another man. I knew there was nothing I could or would do about it, so I busied myself in the kitchen with my girlfriends, trying to forget about him. But while I was busy making sandwiches and fixing drinks, I remembered how fired up I was, bustling all over the place, enjoying the turn on."

That was containment. She was channeling her excitement in an appropriate way under the circumstances, while sustaining her energy.

After you and your partner have each experienced the passive and active roles in the front caress, stop again to talk about the feelings that have been evoked.

At the next practice session do the front caress again, this time including the breast and genitals, but only casually. Touch the entire front of the body, giving

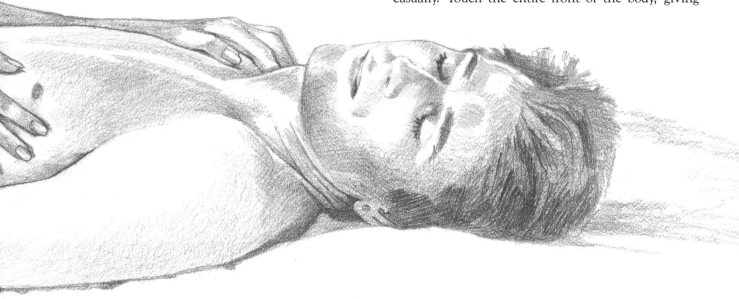

everything a chance to wake up. Touch the breasts and genitals the same way you touch a hand or a face. One is no more important than the other. It would be naive to suggest that being touched will not excite you and sexually charge certain parts of your body. There is nothing wrong with that; it feels delicious. Enjoy it for what it evokes in you. But the purpose of this exercise is to place no more emphasis on the breasts and genitals than you do the head or foot.

When you are the passive partner and you start to feel the urgency building, the body begins to demand greater sexual stimulation. This is your cue to slow it down and study what it feels like while you are building. To stop the urgency, remove your focus from the stimulated sexual areas and think instead about a non-sexual part of your body. Focus on your arm, or the palm of your hand, or your lower leg. This places the energy elsewhere, temporarily slowing down the genital rush. Once you really learn to do this, you will be in control of your own sexual responses. When you are in charge, you can enjoy the excitement for itself, without being diverted by orgasm.

Once again, you achieve more by going slowly, by not rushing from beginning to end. Remember that the enjoyment of an ice cream cone is in the repeated sweetness that comes from every lick, and the crunchiness of each bite of the cone. When you rush to finish it in five minutes you are disappointed that it is gone. Something is missed by rushing. When we receive a lovely rose, we take care of it hoping that it will stay colorful and fragrant, so that we may enjoy it for as long as possible. It is no different with your sexual experiences.

When you are the active partner, pay attention to your partner's responses. Remember what caused him to react in a certain way. What set off his erection or

caused his nipples to harden? This knowledge will be useful to both of you later on.

Spend about twenty minutes in each role, stopping to share feelings before the role switch and then again afterward. Compare notes on how it felt and what the differences were between the first and second times. Did you prefer oil or powder? Was the first caress more relaxing or less relaxing than the second? As you felt your partner's hand lightly brushing your breast did it feel comforting, or not intense enough to satisfy you? Were you frustrated to have your genitals touched as casually as your shoulder? You can learn a lot about your own sexuality from this exercise and the conversation following it. Take time to explore those feelings.

After the completed front caress is a good time to practice touch anticipation again, which you learned in the last chapter. While you are lying on your back with your eyes closed, anticipate where the hand will move next on your body. Feel your skin reach out, waiting to be touched. As your partner strokes your thigh, you might begin feeling something stirring in your genital area. This means that as you anticipate, you permit yourself to respond.

As usual, you and your partner take turns in the active and passive roles, talking about the experience before the role change, and then again afterward. Each of you practices maintaining sexual urgency and then slowing it down, to see how much in control you are. The idea is to learn how to create and sustain the feeling you want, where you want it, for as long as you want it. Now you are really in charge of your sexual responses, able to turn them on and off as you wish.

People often have difficulty with containment. A man who has an erection usually feels he must do something about it. A woman who has sexual stirrings may feel that she can only be satisfied through orgasm.

FRONT CARESS

The point of containment is to use the arousal state to benefit you in ways that are not sexual.

As a containment exercise, find a time when you can walk away from a situation where you are about to have an orgasm, and put yourself in a totally different environment. Spend a day in a mild state of arousal and see how brilliant and effective you are at whatever you are doing. You may be more productive at work, or you may decide to do the spring cleaning you have been avoiding. Whether you catch up on your letter writing or go bike riding with your children, you are exercising your right to feel good.

There are times when containment is essential to appropriate behavior. It is not uncommon for the father of a teenage daughter to become aroused at the sight of her in a sexy bikini, and there really is nothing wrong with the feeling. It is a biological response to an attractive sight. There is no need for guilt or withdrawal. At the same time, there is no need for him to do anything about the feelings or to fear them. He can enjoy them for what they are and take pride in his lovely offspring. Containment is a healthy and constructive life skill.

You can enjoy the front caress in a casual way or as a prelude to foreplay and intercourse. Learning to appreciate touch as a fulfillment unto itself accords you the choice as to whether or not you want sex to be the outcome. A frequent complaint among women is that men feel that every physical encounter must end in orgasm. Many women themselves have a sense of incompletion without it. But there are several ways to feel satisfaction; and orgasm is only one of them.

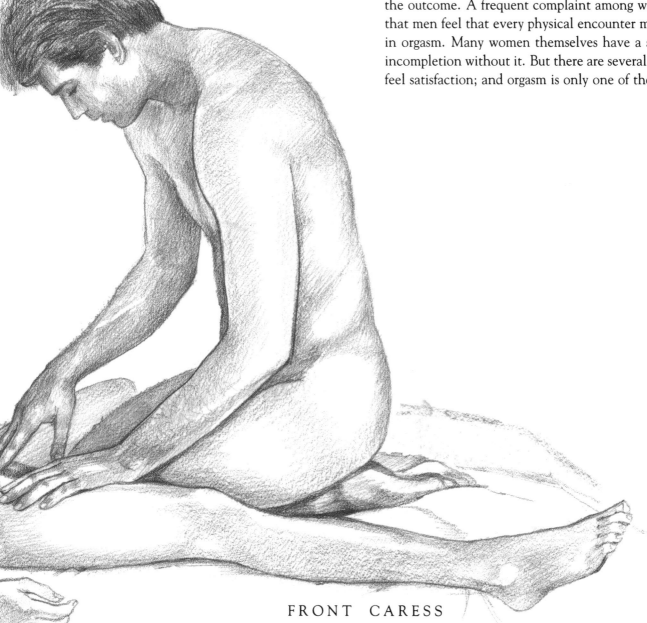

FRONT CARESS

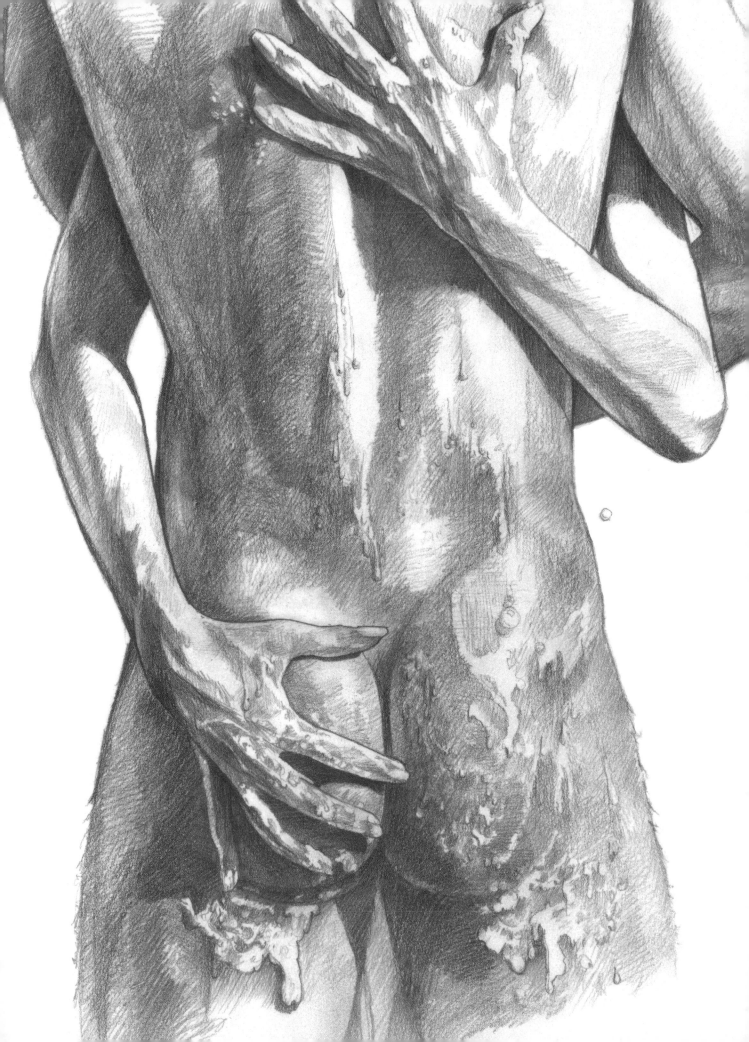

SENSUAL SHOWER

In the 1960s, during a severe water shortage, a wonderful slogan was sweeping the country, "Save water, shower with a friend." It seemed like a good idea at the time, and a noble contribution to water conservation. Have you ever tried it? There is a significant difference in the bathing experience when you are with a partner who can caress your wet and soapy body all over. The shower becomes more than just an exercise in cleanliness and daily habit.

We would like to introduce you to the "sensual shower" as we know it, and have you enter yet another phase of this journey through touch.

The entire body has been caressed now, leaving no parts untouched. You have seen and felt every inch of yourself and your partner. The sensual shower provides another arena in which to explore and caress each other from head to toe, back and front.

Before you take a shower with your partner, do it alone, without the intrusion of someone else. Of course we have all taken showers before, but the sensual shower is not like a typical five-minute scrub before leaving for work in the morning, or a quick rinsing off before going to sleep. The sensual shower takes one hour. It is necessary to give yourself this time so that you can experience bathing in a new way.

Prepare your environment, making it serene and romantic, even though you are alone. Turn the lights off, light a candle, and play music softly in the background. Keep the bathroom warm. These are only sug-

8

The significance lies in the fact that you have taken the time to nurture yourself

gestions, and perhaps you will think of other ways to enhance the environment for yourself.

Once you step inside the shower enclosure, stop thinking about your problems, your children, your next appointment, or whatever else ordinarily has you rushing to get out in a few minutes. Set aside the hour and know that you are dedicating this time to yourself and your own pleasure. Be fully present in this shower, with the understanding that getting clean is only the by-product; feeling good is the reason.

Feel the heat of the water warming your body as it glides over your hair and skin. Adjust the pressure according to your taste, but all you really need is enough water to keep the soap from drying. It can be as little as a trickle. Choose a soap that is both fragrant and creamy, so that your sense of smell as well as touch is being gratified. Once again, concentrate on different areas of your body and isolate the various feelings for your own information and pleasure. How do your hands feel when they are slippery? How does your shoulder react to a soapy hand on it? In the small confines of a shower cubicle, it will be easier for you to focus than ever before. Use the space to your advantage and tune into yourself completely.

Now you are being truly good to yourself. Treating yourself well goes beyond buying nice clothes or a fancy car. They are superficial accoutrements that provide fun and glamour. Being good to yourself on this level means taking responsibility for getting your needs met.

Single or partnered, pleasure from another person is not always available at the moment you may need or want it. As you gently lather your body all over, enjoy the fact that your skin does not know or care who is touching it; it responds favorably to any pleasing touch, including your own.

When your hour is up, you may find that you are somewhat mesmerized from both the length of time you have spent in water and from the mist that has built up around you. Enjoy the euphoria. Step out of the shower slowly, allowing your body to adjust to the change of environment. The shower is truly a testimony to our amphibious nature.

Gently pat yourself dry with a large, soft towel, using it to caress your skin further. Next, take lotion or powder and apply it to your body until you are totally blanketed in softness and fragrance. Regardless of your busy schedule, it would be very difficult at this time to find fault with the hour you have just given to yourself. You have become more intimate with your body on another dimension, and now you are ready to include those feelings with a partner.

As always, you both alternate in the active and passive roles, but there is no conversation at all during this exercise. The shower is totally nonverbal. If you have chosen to start in the active role, begin by soaping your partner's back very slowly, building up a creamy lather. Because you are standing behind your partner you have a lot of room for creativity in your touching. You can continue to use your hands, or you can use your chest to caress his back. Try turning back-to-back and see how it feels to slither up against another soapy body. There really is no rigid format to follow in terms of what part of your body you use to touch or how you touch. If you become aroused, let it happen. Just enjoy the arousal, using containment to help you stay in the sensuality of the moment.

The next step is to reach around to the front of your partner's body, enjoying the contact of your inner arms as you explore his anatomy from head to toe. Bend down, stand on your toes, and do whatever you need to do to touch your partner everywhere, soaping and lathering as you caress. Avoid soaping the face, as the

eyes and mouth may not respond too favorably. If in your travels you come across an erect nipple or penis, enjoy it casually; when you are ready to move on, do so. Go very slowly with this exercise, so that you feel everything, keeping in mind that the shower is not for sexual stimulation but for sensual arousal.

Once you both have had a chance in each role, face one another and put your arms around each other, gently hugging. If you last took the passive role, take a turn now being active. Using your feet, stroke your

partner up and down. How do the bottoms of your feet feel as they slide across his body? As you lather his body all over, lather your own, and then let the water wash the slippery feeling away. Notice the difference in how your skin feels with and without soap. Let your partner take his turn lathering you and exploring as you have just done, and then both of you mutually soap and caress each other. Shampooing each other's hair is an optional treat.

When you are both ready to leave the shower, step out and take turns patting each other dry. Wrap each other in towels and hug closely, feeling the warmth of your two bodies. Apply powder or lotion all over the body. Do this slowly, as you are still pleasuring each other. Dry each other's hair and wrap your heads in towels. This time spent after the shower gives you both an opportunity to be pampered in a very special way.

Whether you enjoy showers because they open up your sensuality, or because they may lead to mad, passionate lovemaking, you have ultimately benefited from this liquid touch adventure. The significance does not lie in a particular outcome, but in the fact that you have taken the time to nurture yourself.

"Showering—even showering alone—has taken on a whole new meaning to me. It's no longer just an act of cleanliness but has become an extraordinary treat. It's a refuge from the pressures of the day. It's a time to relax. It's so warm and loving. Even when I'm forced to take a quick shower, I'm completely aware that it is a sensual experience, and that I am giving it to myself because I deserve it."

The sensual shower is an ideal vehicle for establishing intimacy between two people. Very often women will shy away from showering with a friend, for fear their makeup will run or disappear. Or a man might be concerned about having to remove his hairpiece. Facades can be intrusive; they create distance between people. It would be best to forget your vanity, because it can diminish your potential for pleasure.

The other obvious result of taking a shower is that you have gotten clean. Hygiene is an important part of self worth, of feeling attractive, of pleasure, and of sex; and it needs some special mention. Since you have just left the shower, here is some information about keeping your body clean, healthy, and appealing to your partner.

Brushing and flossing teeth makes for a sweeter and tastier kiss. Deodorant helps to keep your underarms smelling nice. Keep ears soft and free of exterior wax by using a washcloth to clean them and some oil to prevent scaling. If your skin tends to dry out, get in the habit of moisturizing your entire body.

During menstruation, it is particularly important to spread the vaginal lips and clean around them with soap and water, rinsing well. Blood easily lodges in the pubic hair and can become crusty and hard. Additionally, over a period of time, dried blood will have an unpleasant odor. After a menstrual period many women douche as they feel they need a good inside cleaning. This is perfectly acceptable, unless you have been advised otherwise by your physician. Avoid unnatural douche products, especially those with perfume added. Perfume in the vagina is both irritating and unnecessary. Lukewarm water is generally sufficient, unless there is a medical problem. If you are concerned with odor, add a teaspoon of baking soda. If you are feeling irritation, add some plain yogurt. They are both harmless.

In your daily hygiene, don't forget to go inside the vaginal lips to clean away the collection of vaginal secretions and clitoral smegma. It is wise to keep this in check, as it can result in discomfort or even pain, especially during intercourse. An uncircumcized man needs to pull back the foreskin covering the head of his penis and wash away the smegma. Personal hygiene is a reflection of how you feel about yourself.

Some women shave their armpits and legs and occasionally their pubis. There is no right or wrong; do whatever makes you feel best. Fingernails, though beautiful when long and groomed, sometimes hinder sexual activity. If you are going to penetrate your partner at any time with a finger, keep your nails short, clean, and smooth. A long nail inside a vagina or anus is unpleasant as well as potentially damaging to the tender tissue. The time spent in attending to hygiene and grooming can make a difference in the quality of your relationships, experiences, and sense of self.

SEXPLORATION

9

Lead me not into
temptation
I can find it
myself

■■■■■■■■■

Throughout the ages there have been jokes, songs, poems, and books written about the differences between men and women. The supposed gender distinctions are not only anatomical, but emotional, psychological, intellectual, spiritual, and sexual. Most people have accepted these myths, which have evolved into a "male vs. female" platform. There is a critical need to explore the two sexes in a more detailed way, to better understand what it is that separates men and women and what it is that attracts them to each other. We are concerned with similarities, not just differences.

During the body image exercise you stared at your anatomy and allowed your partner to do the same. You progressed to touching all over, including casual caressing of the genitals. Now it is time to complete your examination of both your body and your partner's.

The sexploration exercise is a physiological exploration of your sexual being. It is intended to demythify much that has been erroneously accepted as truth. It is a technical-sexual approach to familiarizing yourself with the human body, taking the mystery out of the sex organs and sexual response as it is experienced by both women and men.

Being intimately familiar with the details of the body you are touching is a pathway toward touching it better and more purposefully. It further acquaints you with the common responses that, when shared, bring you to great sexual heights.

You and your partner should each do your self-examination alone. When you feel comfortable and secure about the location of all your parts, then you will introduce them to your partner.

For genital self-examination, the woman will need a mirror and a flashlight. Both of you will also need a light mineral oil for part of the examination.

As you explore your body, be particularly aware of pleasure responses and their sources. Certain areas of the body for both men and women are "hot spots." You are looking for these areas, as they are instrumental in sexual response. Although other areas are less directly related, they are just as important to your erotic experience.

Anatomic awareness is essential to maintaining good health and good sex. Those areas that bring pleasure to you and your partner are worth finding and remembering. You certainly would not go very far in your car if you had no idea where the ignition or gas tank were. You need basic information about your physiology, and then you will be able to guide even the most naive and resistant of partners.

We will start the self-examination with instructions for the woman. Although you have been nude for several of the exercises, your breasts were touched only casually in the preceding one. At this time hold one of your breasts in your hand and become familiar with every aspect of it. Is it soft, small, full, or low-hanging? Is your nipple inverted, jutting out, large, or small? Is the area around the nipple—the areola—large, dark, smooth, or shriveled? Your answer will vary depending on the air temperature, time of the month, excitation level, and muscle tone.

How do you like your breasts to be held and touched by a partner? One way to find out is to place the nipple in the palm of your hand and move the breast, lifting up and out. Compare that with the feeling you get when you move your hand down and hard. Some women like their breasts lightly squeezed, while others prefer a stronger grasp. As with any touching, start gently at first, paying close attention to your response.

See how all parts of your breast react to different touches. Softly twirl the nipple between your thumb and middle finger and watch it become hard and erect. As the sensitivity builds, does it seem like your breast is becoming fuller, protruding more? Does the entire breast respond more to vibrating movement or to light stroking? If you squeeze the breast, is it painful? If you push your breasts together so that they are touching, does that excite you? Experiment to see what your particular responses are to stimulation. Include both breasts in your exploration.

The next step gives you the opportunity to examine your genitals close up. Prepare a place where you can sit on a towel or sheet, with pillows arranged comfortably behind your back. Wash your hands before you start. Prop a mirror between your feet, because it is difficult to get a good look at some of the genital area without it.

Now examine the texture of your pubic hair. For some people it is long, straight, and silky. Other vulvas are covered in short, coarse, curly hair. Some women shave their pubic hair because of custom or preference.

Each pubic hair has a nerve ending in the skin. Stroke your pubic hair and notice the special kind of tactile response you have. With both index fingers, stroke up and down the crease of the groin. Now use pressure toward the legs as you halt the stroking. How does that feel? As you press lightly toward the genitals you are closer to the top of the pubococcygeal, or PC muscle. Next, stroke the outer lips, hair, and skin, very lightly and slowly.

After you have become familiar with the outer lips, or labia majora, spread them apart with your fingers, so that you will be able to look at the inner lips, or labia minora. Except when penetration occurs, these lips cover and protect the clitoris and the vaginal and urethral openings.

Use the light mineral oil on your fingertips for the next part of the exploration to avoid any discomfort when rubbing mucous membranes of the vulva and the inside of the vagina. To prevent friction or drying out, keep the area moist while you are examining the area. Run your fingers along the hairline of your outer lips and notice how different this feels from the crease of the thigh. Next, touch the inside wall of the outer lips and notice the spots that respond most. It varies with each individual. In your mirror you can observe the color, texture, and shape. It is fascinating to see your body's many different personalities and looks. Over a period of time you will discover how your body changes in physical appearance depending on variables such as menstrual cycle, pregnancy, age, weather conditions, general health, and sexual stimulus.

Trace all the folds of the outer and inner lips with your fingernails to see if that brings about more feeling. Certain places will respond quicker than others, sending off more pleasure signals. You want to wake up the entire area, paying particular attention to the parts that respond the least. In your mirror, you may notice a change in color of the mucous tissues. This means that you are beginning to become aroused. Sexual feelings may also cause swelling, which is very normal. Vulvas differ in size, shape, color, and texture. When the vulva is opened up, with the lips pulled up and out, it sometimes resembles a valentine.

At the top of the vagina, between the folds of the inner lips, lies the clitoris. Before stimulation it is a pinkish color, typically the size of a pea. It becomes erect through changes in temperature and through stimulation. The clitoris is covered by a hood, or foreskin. This can easily be pulled aside, but it serves as a protection for this sensitive organ. The clitoris is a particularly excitable part of the female anatomy. When stimulated, it often brings a woman to orgasm.

As a woman becomes excited and ready for orgasm, her PC muscle tightens and changes the shape of the vaginal area. The clitoris retracts and becomes covered by the hood. It may appear as though the clitoris has vanished. This is the sign that orgasm is imminent; the body is preparing for the next phase.

This is an ideal time to experiment with clitoral stimulation. Lubricate one or two fingers and gently and slowly caress around and directly on the clitoris. Are you starting to secrete vaginal fluid as your excitation level increases? Do you feel a tightening of the PC muscle as a response to the touching? Is it, in fact, bringing you closer to orgasm, as the erect clitoris receives all this attention? See the value in knowing your body and understanding which areas provide you with the most pleasure. With your partner, this knowledge is invaluable in guiding him.

Take your time studying the details of your genitalia in various stages. Now you are ready to examine the vaginal canal. Touch the top of your pubic bone with a finger, then let it gently slide down into the vaginal opening. Insert your finger a little at a time. Stop and tighten your PC muscle and see what that feels like as it grips your finger. Move in another quarter of an inch, stop and tighten your muscle, again noting the feelings in your vagina. As your finger progresses deeper,

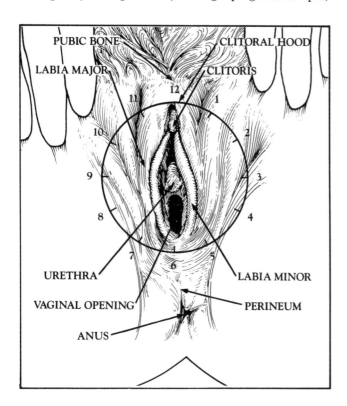

you might notice some lubrication and sexual stirrings. It takes only a third of the index finger to reach the PC muscle to create sensation for the woman.

The PC muscle is a circular structure, much like a three-quarter inch wide rubber band. Imagine that this circle is like the face of a clock. Leave your finger on the PC, lightly pushing up at twelve o'clock. Tighten the muscle. How does it feel? Chances are, not very sexual. At one, two, and three it may not stimulate you much either, even with more pressure. At four, five, six, seven, and eight, however, you may be noticing strong arousal. Squeeze your muscle at each number, to see where your hot spots are. Since everyone's anatomy design differs, it is necessary to experiment with your body to find your own particular sensitivities. The area from nine to twelve may not produce any more excitement than twelve to three, but check anyway. Many women believe that after childbirth, vaginal feeling in their lower section—four to eight—has been numbed by one or more episiotomies. This is possible, because scar tissue often has no feeling. However, women with this problem sometimes find that nature compensates, and the hot spots are found in the upper half, nine through three.

There is no universal rule when it comes to feeling. Your feelings are uniquely yours.

At the bottom of the vaginal canal, lying at a 45° angle, is the cervix. When you touch the cervix it feels something like the tip of a nose. During ovulation and pregnancy, however, it softens. After childbirth, it feels less like a nose and more like a chin.

The appearance of the cervix changes during menstruation, illness, or pregnancy. Using a speculum, your doctor can tell much about your physical state by looking at your cervix. A speculum is a metal or plastic instrument that holds the vaginal canal open, allowing the doctor to see inside. During your next gynecological exam, ask your doctor to let you look.

When you observe the cervix it is like looking straight down at the head of the penis, and it is about the same size. There is a little pinhole-sized opening in the center of the cervix. This is the os, or mouth of the cervix.

It is the opening through which sperm enters the womb and menstruation flows out. In women who have had children, this opening becomes slightly larger, since during childbirth the os opens wide enough to permit the baby to emerge. The mucus in this area becomes watery at the time of ovulation, which makes it easier for the sperm to swim up. At other times of the month the mucus is thicker. If you are checking yourself for health purposes, you might want to smell the secretion to see if it has any unpleasant odor. Odor often signifies infection. You might even taste it, as it is usually taste-free when healthy.

The distance between the vaginal opening and the anal opening is called the perineum. If you have had children you are probably familiar with the perineum area. That is where the doctor, in preparation for the delivery, typically cuts a slit to make the vaginal opening larger. After the child is born, the doctor then repairs the incision; this is called an episiotomy. Some women complain after childbirth that the perineal area has been left desensitized. This is true because surgery can result in decreased feeling because of scar tissue. However, this area is a sexually sensitive one in most women, whether or not they have had children.

During orgasm, some women produce a small amount of clear or milky liquid that is directly related to stimulation of an area known as the Graphenburg Spot, or G Spot. The liquid, once thought to be urine, is now believed to be ejaculate. This is a fairly new concept; not everyone accepts the idea of female ejaculation. Some claim that the liquid is simply a natural lubrication that appears with excitement, and many doctors believe it is urine. The fact that it spurts out of the urethra during the orgasmic spasms has lead many sex researchers to believe otherwise.

Their findings indicate that the female ejaculate has the same compositon as the male ejaculate, with the exception that hers lacks sperm content. There has been considerable resistance to this concept, but there was a time when the idea of female orgasm was not accepted either, and now multiple female orgasm is not only medically recognized but is enjoyed by many women. The stimulated G Spot is instrumental in female multiple orgasm as well as ejaculation. It is considered by some researchers to be the female equivalent of the male prostate gland. The tissue and its location is actually the same in both sexes.

Now, how do you find this elusive spot? It is a place definitely worth finding. First, empty your bladder. Then place your index and middle fingers inside the vagina, beyond the pubic bone. The G Spot is very deep inside, and it is possible that your fingers will not be long enough to reach it. You might try squatting and bearing down. This can make it more accessible. When you feel like you are going to urinate, then you are very close to or directly on the spot. It is a small, spongy tissue past the front wall of the vagina and the urethra. If this highly sensitive area receives friction during intercourse, it becomes swollen and produces sexual feelings that lead to excitation and sometimes orgasm. If it is kept stimulated after orgasm, you will find yourself heading toward another one, and maybe more after that. Sometimes, it requires direct pressure, and at other times gentle rubbing is more effective. Experiment with light and heavy pressure, slow and fast touching, to determine your own needs.

While this is an instructive phase of your program, it should be fun and creative as well. You are permitting yourself to fully explore your body in a way that too often is reserved only for your doctor. When you understand the fact that your body belongs to you, then perhaps your commitment to it will be greater.

Now, here are the self-examination instructions for the man, starting with the breasts. As a man, are you surprised to think of your breasts as an erogenous zone? If so, you have some further exploration to do. The breasts are erotic, whether male or female. There is pleasure for you in breast stimulation, but it may require experimentation, just as we suggested to the woman. At first you may not feel much arousal, but that may be the result of cultural imprinting.

If you have never experienced the feelings of an erect nipple, try wetting your nipples and then blowing on them. This often causes them to harden, and it feels good, too. Try brushing across your nipples with your hand to stimulate them. See if you can discover where your sensitivities are.

Although we are emphasizing the sameness between the sexes, there are of course obvious differences. Among them is the man's ability to create muscles and the woman's ability to develop breasts. Although we sometimes see very muscular female bodybuilders, women do not have the capacity to develop bodies like men. Men likewise do not have the hormones that allow them to develop large breasts. So put any fears to rest about developing larger breasts from having them stimulated, either manually or orally. You will definitely not need a bra from this activity, but you are certainly capable of enjoying the experience.

"A client was doing the body image exercise, and when he got to his breasts, he alluded to them as 'these useless things.' I gave him a little lecture about the breasts and told him how, in some Aborigine cultures, the fathers breastfeed the babies in the mothers' absence. As he looked at me in disbelief, I further suggested that he acknowledge his breasts and their existence. He challenged me, arguing that the breasts are a woman's thing, and why would he waste time on a part of the body that provides no sexual satisfaction for a man. As a young boy he had been taught that only girls have sexual feelings in their breasts.

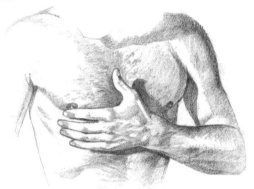

"There goes the imprinting again, further cutting off potential pleasure for the man. So I told my client a story about a former boyfriend of mine. I was just a teenager and was out with him one night. We were kissing and hugging and getting hotter by the minute. He proposed that we have intercourse, but I was not ready for that, so he asked if I would rub his nipples instead. I was surprised but agreed to it, and guess what? He had an orgasm. Here was a man who did not get caught up in gender parameters. He didn't suppress that which he knew to be a good feeling."

Don't miss out on the potential delights of breast stimulation. After you have explored your breasts, continue down to your stomach, pubic bone, and genital area to discover the location of your own hot spots. Begin by touching the corona, or head, of the penis very slowly all around. A light mineral oil will assist in the explorative processes and will help avoid unnecessary irritation. Let your finger glide carefully over the urethral opening. How does that feel? For some men the opening is very sensitive, so be very gentle at first. If the area is rubbed too hard, the feeling will deaden. If you are not circumcized you will need to draw the foreskin back so that you can touch everything on the head of the penis.

Move to the coronal ridge, keeping your eyes closed and touching slowly. Next move your fingers in the crease to the underside, or frenulum; this often generates strong sexual sensation. The skin of a circumcized penis is usually a little tougher and less sensitive. Touch the shaft one section at a time—front, each side, and the underside; then let your fingers slide down the shaft to the base and squeeze gently. Take both testicles and touch, hold, and gently squeeze them; and then again, one at a time. How much pressure do you like? It varies among men; there is no norm. In some men, an erection will result. Explore your perineum area by stroking it. How does that feel?

Notice your pubic hair. Is it soft or coarse? Study your penis. Is it long, short, thick, or narrow? Again, there is no right or wrong shape. Whatever you are is right for you.

A particularly sensitive area of the penis is the raphe. This is the line located on the underside of the penis, beginning under the coronal ridge at the frenulum. It continues between the testicles to the anus as the perineal raphe. Stroke lightly on this line, being aware of how it feels and what response it evokes. Continue along the raphe as it progresses from the base of the penis and perineum to the anal opening.

After you have each explored yourselves alone, it is time to explore together. As you go through the process for a second time, you will remember areas that were particularly sensitive to your touch. You may dis-

SEXPLORATION

cover new ones after being touched by your partner. That's why this is called "sexploration." We are exploring each other's sexual makeup.

When you are examining each other's breasts, you may notice hard and erect nipples. Often this is caused by arousal. Other times it is precipitated by cool air, moisture on the body, or the friction of clothing.

When the man is examining the woman internally, be certain that she is sufficiently lubricated. Women sweat inside the vaginal walls, which produces a flow of secretion that will generally provide adequate moisture. However, depending on a woman's age, her physical health, her mental attitude, and her menstrual cycle, she may not provide sufficient lubrication to avoid irritation when touched. If this is the case, apply light mineral oil or some saliva to the area. Saliva is a natural substance and will not be harmful in any way. Using unnatural products is not recommended, especially ones that contain perfume, which can cause burning. Remember too that a dry vagina is not necessarily indicative of an unexcited woman.

The anus, for some people, is a highly sensitive area, one that when stimulated brings a great deal of sexual pleasure. To others, it is a restricted area.

Get agreement from your partner before you touch the anus. If there are no objections, touch lightly all around the opening. See if that feels good. The skin around the anus is very smooth to the touch.

For much of the body there are no definite rules. That is the reason we take time to study the body with interest. We want to avoid assumptions.

A man displays a fair amount of changes throughout his body at various times. When he becomes excited and ready to ejaculate, his testicles rise from their low-hanging position and move closer to the body. When they are not in a state of arousal they drop down again, as they need to avoid steady contact with normal body temperature. The heat is too intense for the sperm and could destroy the man's fertility.

Don't confuse ejaculation with orgasm. They are not the same, nor do they necessarily occur simultaneously. Ejaculation is the emission of seminal fluid, which fertilizes the female egg. Orgasm is a muscle

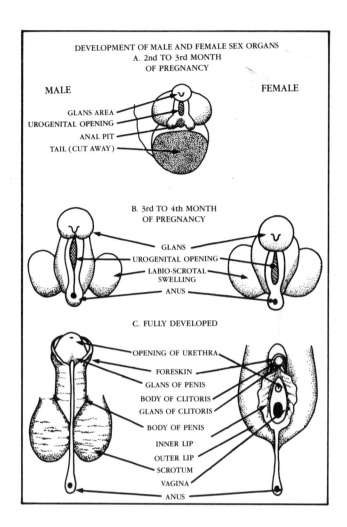

DEVELOPMENT OF MALE AND FEMALE SEX ORGANS
A. 2nd TO 3rd MONTH OF PREGNANCY

MALE   FEMALE

GLANS AREA
UROGENITAL OPENING
ANAL PIT
TAIL (CUT AWAY)

B. 3rd TO 4th MONTH OF PREGNANCY

GLANS
UROGENITAL OPENING
LABIO-SCROTAL SWELLING
ANUS

C. FULLY DEVELOPED

OPENING OF URETHRA
FORESKIN
GLANS OF PENIS
BODY OF CLITORIS
GLANS OF CLITORIS
BODY OF PENIS
INNER LIP
OUTER LIP
SCROTUM
VAGINA
ANUS

spasm, designed to give pleasure.

Earlier we said that we were concerned with the similarities between men and women, not just the differences. It is interesting to note that until the six-week fetal stage, we are all female. At that point, nature redesigns the male fetus. The outer lips join and become the scrotum. The inner lips become part of the foreskin system, which protects the head of the penis. The ovaries move outside the body, settle in the scrotum, and become the testicles. Once we have begun to form according to our gender, we become physically male or female; but we all begin the same. Knowing this may help us to recognize that people are not necessarily alike or different because of a penis or vagina. What is important is not gender or sexual preferences. What is important is how we respond as human beings.

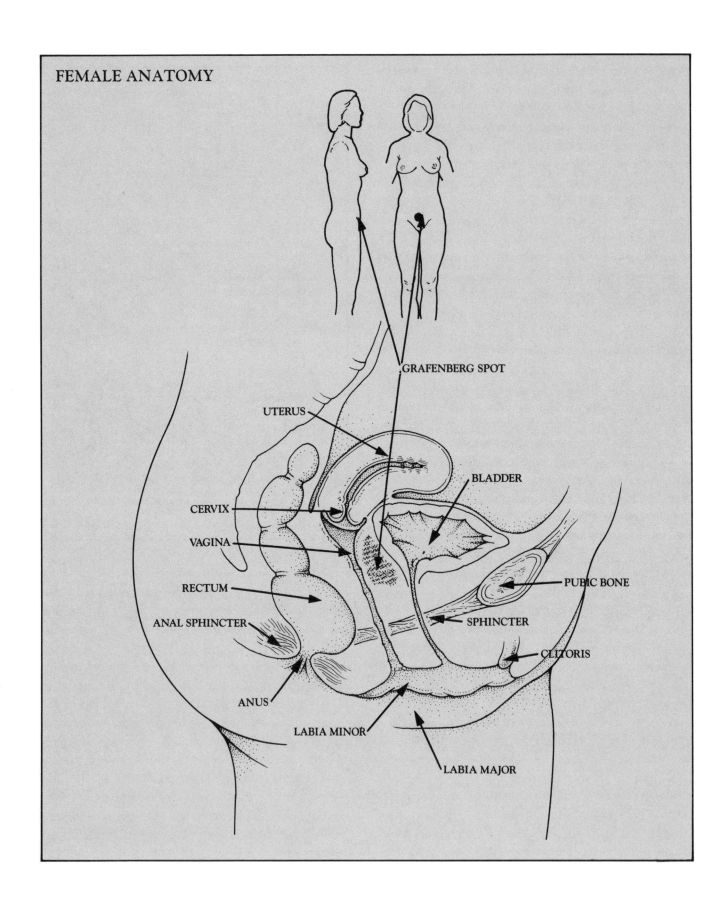

GRAFENBERG SPOT

UTERUS

BLADDER

CERVIX

VAGINA

RECTUM

PUBIC BONE

ANAL SPHINCTER

SPHINCTER

CLITORIS

ANUS

LABIA MINOR

LABIA MAJOR

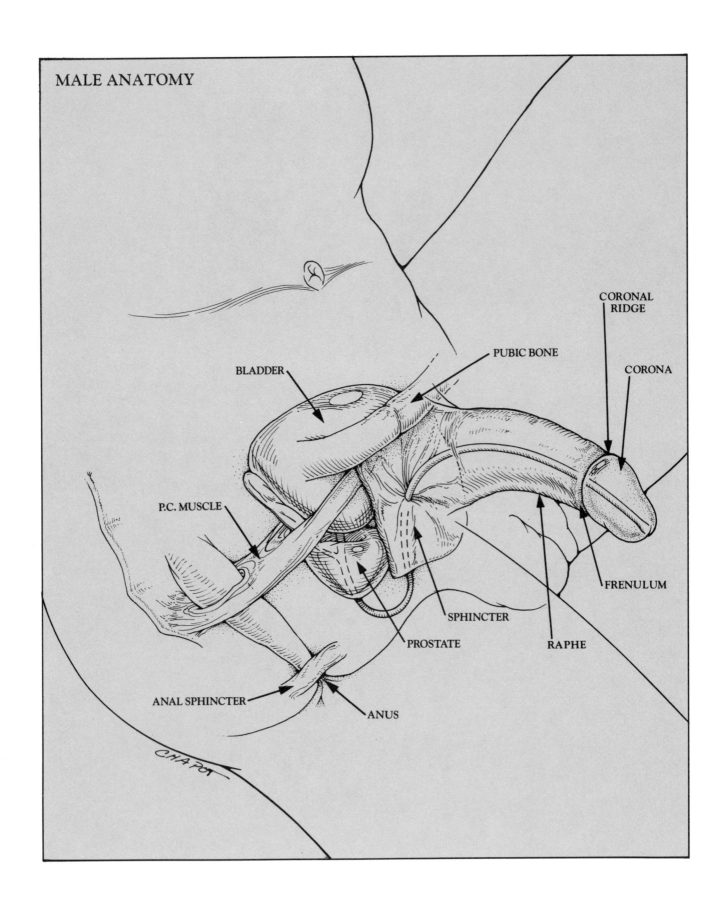

CORONAL
RIDGE

CORONA

PUBIC BONE

BLADDER

P.C. MUSCLE

FRENULUM

SPHINCTER

PROSTATE

RAPHE

ANAL SPHINCTER

ANUS

CHAPOT

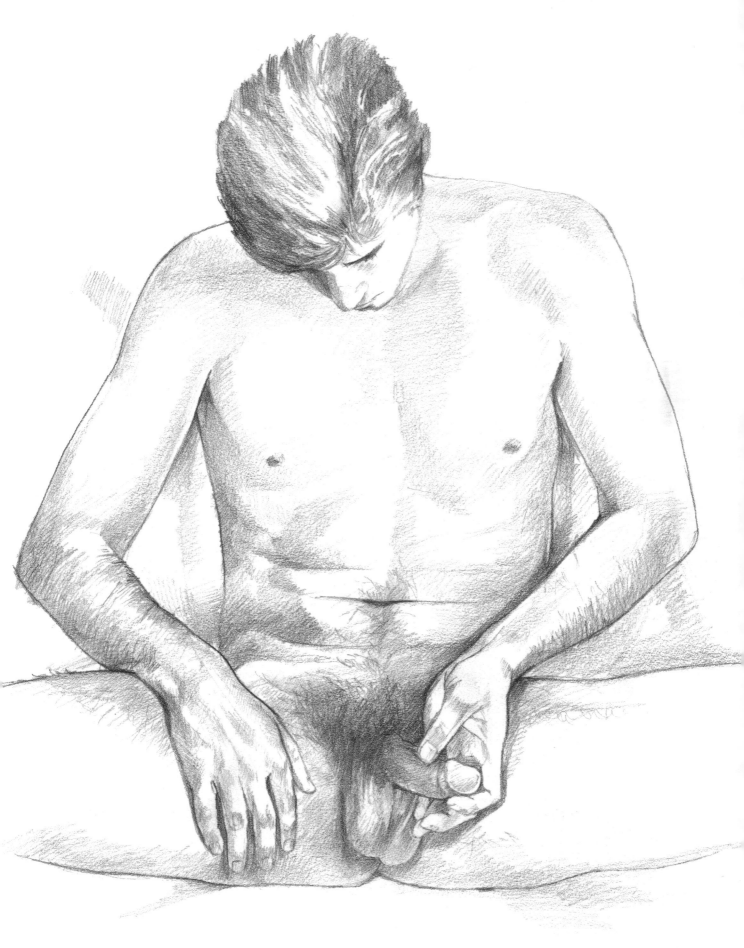

PLEASURING

10

Take the time to feel each caress

"It was summertime, and I decided to take a leisurely drive toward the mountains. There was a lake I had often visited as a child, and I longed to return there once more.

"After serveral hours and several wrong turns, I was lost in the middle of nowhere. Or so I thought. I drove until I found a village and ventured further where I noticed some people in what seemed like a tightly knit group.

"I parked my car and walked over to where the people were, in hopes of getting directions to this lake. All at once, I was met with warm, smiling faces and escorted to a natural pool of water, where people lay sunning themselves.

"Everyone seemed happy and peaceful and extremely affectionate. I didn't want to be rude, but my curiosity got the best of me, and I asked a woman where I was and who they all were.

"'You're in the State of Pleasure, where there is no starvation or loneliness. Welcome.'

"And then she hugged me. Soon others joined us and before I knew it, I was swimming with all these strangers who didn't feel strange. They seemed eager to please me in every way, My body was massaged, my wet hair was combed and dried. I was served fresh fruit and juice, and serenaded by some kind of musical instrument.

"I asked again who the people were and how they all got together, and one man responded finally:

"'We all arrived here because of our individual needs and dissatisfaction with society as we knew it. Our commitment is to feeling the best we can feel during our lifetime and to teach others how to take their pleasure.'

"I really thought I had reached the ultimate in life — a civilization devoted to making the best of every day, in every way. I found myself taking walks, holding hands, lying side by side, and embracing many of the residents — old and young. The children were especially fun. Infants slept peacefully in their fathers' arms. There were no sad faces.

"They invited me to spend the night, and by morning, I knew I had reached Utopia. I had finally found a way to satisfy my need for bonding and physical affection. I would live here forever."

A dream, perhaps, but a good indication of what this woman was holding in her subconscious when she had the dream. Hedonistic lifestyles surface in dreams, where it is safe, but in reality we are criticized if we are pleasure seekers.

Remember that pleasure does not have to be sought after. It is already inside us. We have to merely allow it to be felt.

Taking time with each caress, you have opened up your body to new feelings and responses. This has allowed you to study your partner as well as yourself, increasing your understanding of your mutual sexual needs. During the body image you confronted yourself visually, reducing anxiety about your physical appearance, learning to accept yourself as you are. The sensual shower, like the foot caress, added soap and water and a new sensation to touching. During sexploration, you had the opportunity to recreate the old childhood favorite of "playing doctor."

Foreplay is usually thought of as a prelude to intercourse, frequently becoming only a quick route to orgasm. If you can think of foreplay in a new way, as a total experience of its own, you will have added something of value to your pleasuring repertoire.

The exercises in this chapter are meant to be enjoyable, but they are also a learning aid. In studying them you will become familiar with more of what feels good to you sexually and where you like being touched. You will recognize early signs of arousal, giving you the power to either moderate them or let them evolve naturally. You are learning how to assume even more control of your pleasure, no longer a victim of it.

The pleasuring exercises are to be done once without talking, and then a second time with gestures and conversation. Spontaneous body language and vocalizations such as sighs, hums, or groans are encouraged at all times. If the passive partner experiences discomfort from any action, he can indicate this by shifting his body or gently guiding his partner's hand.

When you are in the active role you are studying what it feels like to be totally in charge, while being respectful of your partner's vulnerability. You may feel the need to ask your partner if you are pleasing him; but instead of conversation, watch his facial expressions, sounds, body tension and release, hand movements and gestures, and arching of the torso, all of which indicate what he is feeling.

When you are in the passive role, give yourself permission to be greedy. Respond to your sexual urgings, while avoiding intercourse. You may feel that you want to ejaculate or have an orgasm, but averting climax is part of the lesson you are learning. Assuming control may be difficult at first, but when you sense that orgasm is near, you can apply techniques to delay it. You are learning and practicing these techniques in the pleasuring exercises so that you will be proficient in them by the time you are actively engaging in intercourse.

The mouth is the beginning of our sexual connection, and kissing is a natural lead-in to the pleasuring exercises that follow. Be alone at first. Your focus throughout will be on what your lips are feeling.

Put one hand softly against your mouth, creating a gentle meeting between the two. Use your lips to explore your hand. Kiss the palms of your hands, moving around to the back of your hands, fingers, and knuckles. Kiss gently, never with pressure. Take your knuckles, one at a time, between your lips. Have you ever tried kissing your shoulder? It feels delicious. Explore inside the crook of your arm, and then glide up and down the inner and outer parts of the arm. Use your tongue, and do not stop if you feel yourself getting aroused; all the more reason to keep on kissing, holding your awareness entirely in your lips. If you have long hair, place it between your lips and whatever you might be kissing. Be aware of the textural differences. Kiss wherever you can reach on your body.

"A fifty-year-old man was referred to me because he had not had an erection in seven years. Upon questioning, he also told me that he avoided kissing at all times. Further investigation revealed that when he was a child his family had frequently told him that he had a 'mean-looking' mouth.

"I studied his mouth and found it to be absolutely normal. His lips were quite thin, but there was nothing about them that would preclude his enjoying kissing.

"He had become so self-conscious over the years about his so-called 'mean mouth' that he had created a pattern of leaving a relationship as the possibility of kissing became imminent. Just an innocent goodnight peck would send him running. He believed that if he disliked his mouth so much, how could anyone else want to kiss him. He had not considered the feeling or the function of his lips, only how they looked.

"I gave him homework to do. He was to spend time caressing his own lips—stroking them, outlining them with his fingers, and then wetting them. As the wetness dried, he was to notice the tingling sensation remaining. At all times, the focus was to be on his lips and nowhere else.

"He diligently applied himself to these exercises. Finally, when he was out on a date and the evening came to a close, he decided to risk a goodnight kiss. What resulted was more than he had even fantasized about. He had his first erection in an interminable seven years, as he reconnected his mouth to the rest of his erotic body."

How sad to think of the years this man had loathed his mouth because of what his parents said about it, but it was wonderful for him when he realized that it wasn't too late to reverse behavior patterns.

Now with your partner, before you begin the pleasuring exercises, start with a prelude of kissing exploration. You made your first contact with your partner's lips during the face caress, but it was done with your fingertips, not your mouth. Remember to relax your

PLEASURING

lips while kissing. As you relax them they become softer, fuller, and more receptive to feeling.

The actual process of kissing is a reaching out with your face in a forward motion, but it is not a full-face push toward your partner. Kissing can be passionate without being aggressive or harsh. You do not want to numb feeling; you want to stimulate. Kiss your partner with little pecks, light and delicate. How do your lips feel nibbling tenderly on his ears, tasting his neck and shoulders? This may very well cause goose bumps to appear on your skin. Now that you are not bound by spatial restrictions, you can kiss your partner anywhere at all. Nothing is out of bounds. Explore his body, with his permission. Feel the real joy a kiss can bring.

Kissing does not have to be serious and passionate all the time. Once you have both practiced being in the active role, be silly, be flirtatious, and have fun. Kissing is a lovely way to begin a pleasuring session.

Some people think that kissing must be done with pursed mouth and closed lips in a very serious manner.

"We were doing a kissing exercise and my client became very tense. He was obviously trying too hard to please me. We were following the rule of no talking, so I couldn't tell him to relax.

"I came up with a crazy idea. Removing my false eyelashes, I pressed them above my top lip, creating a mustache. He was kissing my forehead at the time, and we both had our eyes closed, so he was unaware of what I was doing. He worked his way down to my lips and was suddenly kissing hair. He opened his eyes, and we both burst into uncontrollable laughter.

"Well, humor really broke the ice, and after that his kissing changed."

Whatever this man's reason was for being uneasy about kissing, it disappeared, never to return.

Now another dimension is being added. The pleasuring exercises offer ways of enhancing your sexual enjoyment without intercourse.

There are many positions in which you and your partner can give and receive pleasure. Start with one in which intercourse is not possible. Your partner lies on his back and bends his knees, his feet resting on the bed. You sit facing him, with your straight legs extended under his bent knees. Move up as close as

possible to his body, so that his legs are comfortably resting on your thighs. You are in a position where you can reach his whole body, free to touch him everywhere.

Your partner's eyes are closed, and he is relaxing into your touch. You may caress any part of him, starting with his head, neck, and outstretched arm. Casually caress his breasts, stomach, genitals, legs, and feet, with no particular pattern or emphasis. Randomly keep repeating the caressing for a while longer, to awaken all the skin. Now focus the touch from the extremities toward the genitals. As your partner's hands and arms are being stroked, his nipples may begin to harden in anticipation of further touch; so might yours. Move the energy down his shoulders and stomach into his pubic area, slowly caressing his groin, waking up his penis in anticipation of being touched next. Do this again, this time starting at the feet, caressing upward, stopping at the genitals.

Take his penis in your hand and begin with a light, gliding motion up and down its shaft and around the coronal ridge. With your fingertips, slide along the raphe to the base. Add lubrication, using either saliva or light mineral oil. Explore the area from the penis to the anus, and stroke the anal opening with one or two fingers until you feel it relax. You might insert part of a lubricated finger, being mindful of your partner's comfort. Watch for signs. If he tenses his anal sphincter muscles, or he winces, carefully remove your finger.

If you decide to continue your caress, you will want to wash off your hands before applying them to another part of the body. This is particularly important for a man when he is penetrating a woman anally, either with his penis or finger. The E Coli bacteria found in the anus belongs there, but are incompatible with the vagina and can cause vaginal infection. The man's urethral opening is also vulnerable to the bacteria; he can protect himself against possible infection by using a condom when having anal intercourse.

When you switch positions, with you lying down and your partner sitting up, the procedure will be very much the same. Randomly at first, his caressing will progress from your hands, arms, and shoulders to the breasts, moving the energy down the stomach to the

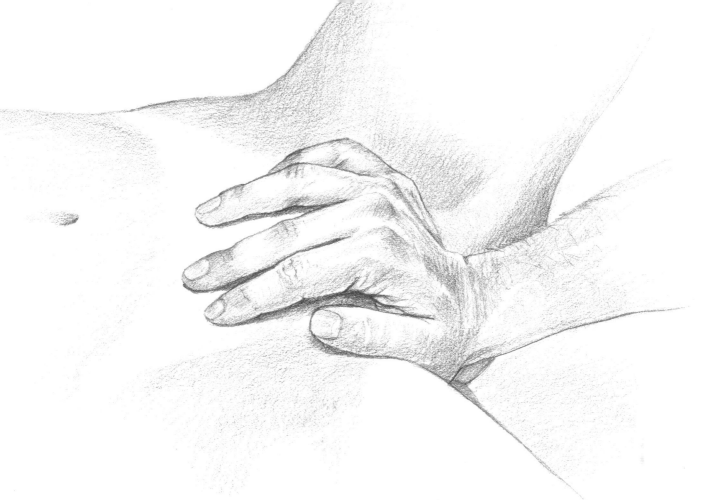

pubic area. Then proceed from the feet, legs, and hips, stopping at the genitals. You may begin to feel a rippling right above the pubic bone, which is an indication of sensual feelings becoming sexual. You may start to move your head from side to side or gyrate your hips as your clitoris is touched and your vagina is filled with finger penetration. The body language continues.

Remember that the person touching must caress toward the genitals. The receiver stays focused on the movement toward the genitals, maintaining the energy there. To slow down the sexual excitement, the active partner caresses away from the genitals. The receiver refocuses, diverting the energy and diffusing it back into the rest of the body.

When you are the active partner, you can watch your lover's movements. At the start, only the passive person's eyes are closed. After you are more familiar with each other's bodies and responses, you will both be able to keep your eyes closed, providing greater focus for your feelings. Listen to your partner's breath-

ing as it becomes more rapid with increased excitement. Notice the difference between passive and active breathing. If the breathing does not become more rapid as your partner approaches orgasm, it may indicate that he is now able to control his sexual buildup. After a while, join your partner's breathing pattern, creating a rhythm. Notice tightened leg muscles, testicles rising closer to the torso, erect nipples, or a tensing of the whole body. This almost certainly indicates increased sexual excitement.

If the woman is at the point of orgasm, the man presses the heel of his hand against her clitoris. Due to the heavy pressure on the nerves, the vibrations will cease and the urgency of her orgasm will diminish. This can be repeated as many times as necessary, until such time as the orgasm is appropriate. Additionally, the man diverts her sexual attention by having her follow his hand as it moves across her skin, away from the genitals and toward the extremities. This technique helps a woman avoid immediate orgasm and

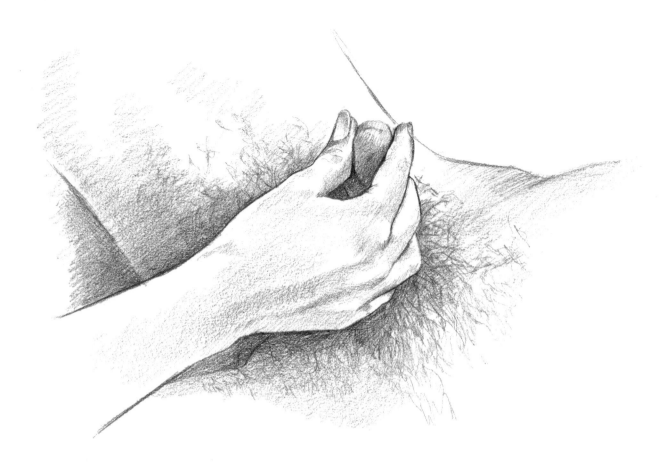

ultimately creates a stronger one. The more she is brought to that level of excitation and then stopped, the more intense and gratifying will be her orgasm.

The fear of premature ejaculation causes anxiety in many men. There are several ways a woman can help her partner prolong ejaculation and orgasm. The most common is the squeeze technique. The woman places her thumb on the frenulum of the penis, with two fingers on the dorsal side, one above and the other below the coronal ridge. She squeezes tightly, and he tightens his PC muscle. The pressure will not hurt an erect penis, only a flaccid one. The squeeze and PC tension is maintainined for ten to fifteen seconds, or until his urgency subsides somewhat. Then they can relax and return to stimulation without immediate worry of orgasm or ejaculation.

After mastering the squeeze technique you can learn a method that will be excellent later, when you study the chapter on intercourse. This technique gives the man the advantage of not having to withdraw from the vagina or anus. In this method the woman squeezes the penis at its base and the man tightens his PC muscle. Once PC muscle control is achieved, tensing that muscle may be all that is needed to avoid ejaculation. The control now rests with the man, and he is no longer at the mercy of his aroused state. Later in this chapter you will be given specific exercises for strengthening the PC, sometimes called the love muscle.

As a man becomes excited his testicles begin to rise, and another way to decrease his arousal is for the woman to very gently take his testicles in her hand to keep them from ascending. This requires extreme delicacy, as he will be feeling quite sensitive to touch.

Some men try to delay ejaculation by thinking away from sex. They concentrate on baseball, work, or anything else nonsexual. We discourage this strategy, since it sabotages his sexual pleasure and his learning process. Instead, applying the deep breathing exercises described earlier, or tightening his PC muscle will help him maintain concentration on his body.

None of these methods is foolproof, and it may be that you or your partner will be unable to intervene quickly enough to avert climax. If you do slip over the edge into orgasm it just means that you need more practice. Experiment with each of the techniques to decide which one has the greatest effectiveness for you, and then practice it several times until you both gain control. Being in control gives you greater freedom with your body while minimizing the chances of premature response.

In the sexploration chapter we discussed the PC muscle and its importance in enhancing sexual pleasure. Like any other muscle, it can be developed to become stronger and more effective. If you are still uncertain as to which muscle it is, try urinating and then momentarily stopping the flow in the middle. The muscle you tighten is the PC. The value of PC control extends to both men and women.

During intercourse, if a woman contracts her PC muscle around her lover's penis, both will experience increased stimulation and arousal. This may bring him to orgasm sooner, but with sufficient communication between partners, this contraction movement can be halted at any time. The advantage of using the love muscle is that it helps to create and keep the erection. This is best appreciated after male ejaculation has taken place and both partners want to continue making love. It is possible that the woman's PC stimulation at that time will again arouse both of them sufficiently to resume their lovemaking.

Exercising the PC muscle is particularly important for a woman after childbirth, because it helps strengthen the area that has been weakened during delivery. It is not uncommon for a new mother to be concerned about her ability to please her partner, fearing that she is no longer able to provide a tight grip for his penis. There is no reason why the couple cannot resume having rewarding sex after the recuperative time during which intercourse is prohibited. Those weeks can be used to regain strength and control through exercise.

For a man, a strong PC muscle is a pathway to controlling ejaculation, which has great value for more reasons than simply prolonging intercourse. Recent studies report that when ejaculation is stalled repeatedly, the sexual buildup becomes so intense that when orgasm finally occurs, it is felt on a much stronger and deeper level. Additionally, increasing numbers of men are experiencing more than one orgasm through PC control, although multiorgasmic response was once erroneously believed to be confined to women only. Though ejaculation usually takes place only once, the contraction of his PC muscle can sometimes cause the man recurring orgasms. This is not a capability he is likely to acquire instantly, but it is essential that he knows that the possibility exists.

Men have not been multiorgasmic because they have been told they were incapable of it. They have been assured that their sexual encounter ends at ejaculation. Investigating the potential of the man's PC muscle can help eliminate some of the many restrictions that have been a result of inadequate information.

There are three basic exercises that you and your partner can each do to strengthen your love muscles. The first is to tighten your PC and hold the contraction for one second; contract once quickly and more intensely, just before release. Repeat the contraction, holding this time for two seconds. Continue repeating, holding one second longer each time, until you are holding for a twenty-second duration. Between contractions, let the muscle come to a complete state of rest. This allows it to gain strength for each following contraction. You will notice that the pelvic area feels warm at each contraction, and that subtle sexual interest is stirring.

While it is important to be able to control the tensing of the PC muscle, it is equally important to control the relaxation of it. You will not be able to hold the contraction (and still control the release) for more than a few seconds when you first begin practicing. Don't tire the muscle by overexercising it. Practice holding it a little longer each day and give the muscle a chance to build up.

The second exercise is similar except that the squeezing and releasing of the muscle is done as rapidly as you can, creating a flutterlike effect. This results in complete tension, followed by total release.

A third exercise follows a push-and-pull pattern. Breathe in deeply while contracting the muscle, and draw in an imaginary object. After holding this position for a few seconds, push out, as if you were expelling this object from your body. Then breathe out and relax. While a woman will draw in from her vagina, a man can draw in from his anus. Practice all three of these exercises for a few weeks, and you will notice increased control and greater sexual pleasure.

You may also observe a "sex flush" on parts of the body. It is a reddish rash on the breasts, lower stomach, face, or neck, a temporary response to excitation that can be seen in many fair-skinned men and women.

Soon you will learn what every change and movement means, as well as every sigh and moan. Encourage the passive partner to feel free to express himself vocally. This is a time to let all the feelings flow into you and out again, according to both of your needs, as you breathe together.

Use these exercises as a key to finding your own pleasure. Show each other what you like and how you like it. Masturbating in front of each other is an effective and often stimulating way to indicate your sexual preferences. When someone is able to watch you do to yourself what you would like done, he is in a better position to fulfill you. There is less guesswork involved. Your partner may become aroused from the experience; this is an added bonus. Masturbating together can be both provocative and informative, making you both feel more intimate as you share your secret worlds.

Masturbating teaches you about yourself as you discover your most sensitive and responsive parts. The knowledge that you can give yourself pleasure alleviates feelings of anxiety and desperation at times when a partner is not available. Making yourself feel good ultimately increases your potential for being a better and more sensitive lover. Furthermore, when you decide to have a sexual encounter with your partner, it will not be out of dependency, but motivated by real desire.

When pleasuring with your partner, if one position is not suitable to the moment or situation, change it. Try the spoon position with sexual stimulation. Lie on your sides facing each other, fondling and talking. Study

each other's faces and notice the change of expression as your hands begin to touch the genitals.

The final exercise we recommend is to enjoy foreplay for all it encompasses, and to stop as orgasm draws near. Get dressed and walk away, taking your sexual feelings with you. You have just learned what it feels like to make love without intercourse. Sometimes intercourse is not possible, even though caressing and lovemaking are. This exercise teaches you to love and appreciate all the different aspects of physical contact, understanding that every component equally contrib-

utes to your sexual wholeness and emotional satisfaction. This exercise also prepares you for "bedlam interruptus," when the unexpected visitor rings your bell, the baby starts howling, or the wakeup alarm and telephone go off at the same time.

We would be remiss if we discussed pleasuring without mentioning oral lovemaking. It is a complete experience of its own. You have done the kissing exercises, but they were not designed to be specifically sexually stimulating. You have explored your partner's anatomy with your hands, inside and out, and now you can do that with your mouth and tongue.

Moving from the extremities inward, use your tongue as you would your hand, touching the body gently and slowly. There are no rules other than the usual hygienic guidelines of making sure you are clean all over. Let your partner flick his tongue around and over your clitoris and in and out of the vaginal opening, while stimulating the G Spot with his fingers. He can con-

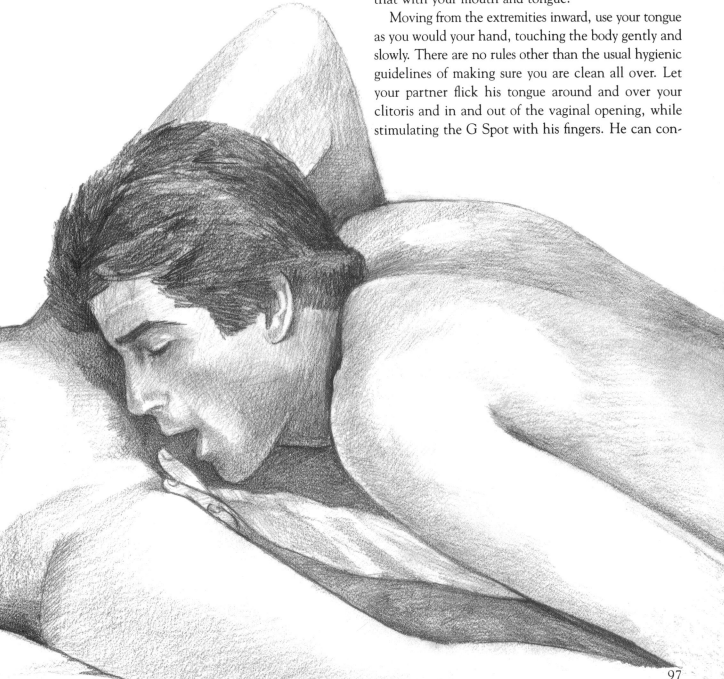

tinue planting kisses on your clitoris as he penetrates the anus with a finger. Sucking the clitoris into his mouth intermittently, he is also free to reach up to the nipples, licking and biting them gently.

Oral sex is much the same for men and women, with the exception of the differences in anatomy. You can draw your partner's penis into your mouth, sucking lightly or hard depending on his preference. Be careful of your teeth as you glide up and down the penis, as the sharp edges can scratch. Some men enjoy having their testicles sucked, while others find the pressure too intense. Be sure you know what your partner wants.

Swirl your tongue around the top ridge of the penis, down the raphe to the perineum. Hold the testicles in your hand, tenderly caressing them, as you proceed with your tongue to the anal area. Penetrate the anus with your tongue, moving it in and out slowly. It is necessary to wash the tongue after it has been in the anus before inserting it into a mouth or vagina. It is a good idea to save anal stimulation for last whether you are using fingers, tongue, or penis, since it is distracting to stop what you are doing in order to wash.

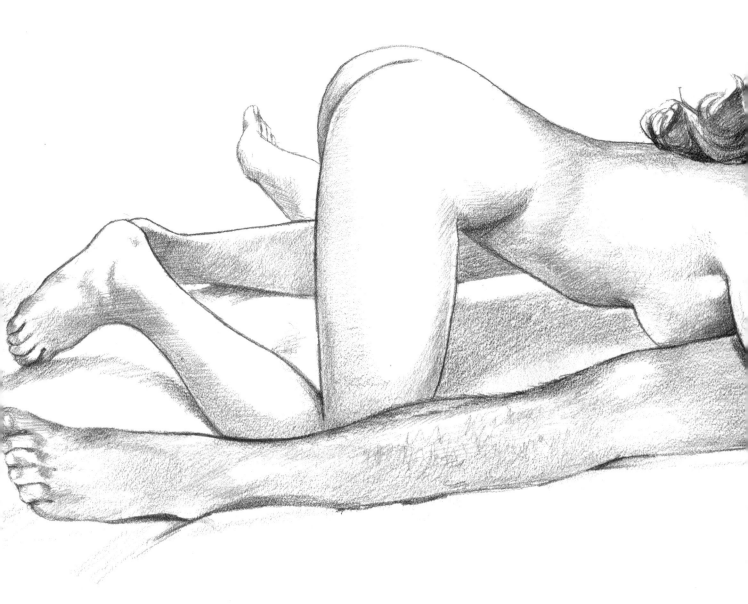

PLEASURING

A great advantage to oral sex is that it can follow intercourse. There may be times when the erection is gone but the desire remains, and the lovemaking can continue orally. It gives you more time to caress and enjoy each other. Also, it is not unusual for the erection to return after genital kisses have been exchanged.

The variety of ways in which you experience sensual and sexual stimulation and excitation change constantly. Be aware of your choices, love what you are doing each moment, and you can and will have it all.

PLEASURING

99

INTERCOURSE

11

Once the wheel of love has been set in motion there is no absolute rule

Frank Sinatra once sang a song with lyrics that were to have a great impact on lovers everywhere: "When somebody loves you, it's no good unless he loves you, all the way." Going "all the way" was something nice girls only fantasized about in the 1950s, and it was not until the decades following that "going all the way," or sexual intercourse, was openly talked about and debated. Today, our society has come to recognize the value of intercourse beyond that of making babies.

Perhaps the most desired stage of lovemaking, intercourse is to many people the highest goal in sexual fulfillment. But like many other pleasuring taboos, it has been surrounded by myths and exaggerations. Intercourse is another way of touching. It is intimate, private, and different, as is the caress of a mother to her child or the touch given to comfort a friend.

We are by no means attempting to deny the beauty of intercourse by giving it equal status with other forms of touch. There is no argument that this level of sexual exchange is very special, allowing two people to be as physically close as possible through penetration of the penis into the vagina. What happens during that closeness is a mutual bonding that lasts for at least as long as the duration of their lovemaking. It is an act that evokes a wide range of emotions, and it is preferably based on trust and respect.

The degree to which intercourse brings you pleasure has much to do with how well you integrate all prior steps of the program as enhancement for this final step. Incorporate all that you have learned thus far and you will make love with a far greater appreciation for the human body and a higher respect for its basic need: to be touched.

As with all the other steps, we shall lead you to this last step gradually, starting with a warm-up exercise called *quiet penetration*. The male lover may now penetrate the woman with his penis for one hour, but neither partner may thrust or talk for the duration. The lesson is to savor sensual communication without embellishment such as talking, moving, looking, hearing, or smelling. We suggest that the man begin with a flaccid penis rather than an erect one, although we recognize that this is not always easy to do. If the penis is erect, it will gradually become flaccid if neither partner thrusts after insertion.

Beginning with a flaccid penis teaches the man and woman that an erection is not essential for penetration, and therefore a flaccid penis should not deter or discourage them from intercourse. If the penis is placed behind the woman's PC muscle, the natural gripping of the muscle in its normal state will usually keep the penis from slipping out. This is another lesson in containment. We discourage thrusting, ejaculation, and orgasm, as they interfere with what you are learning now. Your focus is on the moment, without proceeding to the orgasmic state. This requires concentration and the possible utilization of one of the delay techniques you have learned to avoid ejaculation and orgasm.

There is much to be gained from lying quietly together. You will begin to notice subtle nuances that are often missed during the active state of thrusting.

INTERCOURSE

For the man, how does it feel to penetrate your lover with a flaccid penis? Does it feel more gentle and tender? Are you less sexually aroused? You are probably more conscious of the total body and less focused on the genitals than you would be during active sexual relations. You are closely connected to each other and are taking the time to savor it.

As a woman, what is it like to be penetrated by a soft penis? Are you more aware of your PC muscle than you generally would be during thrusting? Is it fun to caress your lover slowly and with interest while he penetrates your vagina? Be aware of your urge to thrust and simply enjoy it.

There are several particularly good positions for quiet penetration. Be certain that your bodies are very close to each other so that the penetration is possible.

You are both in the spoon position, the woman in front, the man penetrating her vagina. Adjust your bodies to find the angle most comfortable for you.

From the basic spoon position, with the woman in front, the man remains still while the woman turns on her back, perpendicular to her partner. She then lifts her legs and places them over his lap. She is sitting on his lap while laying down, making her vagina totally available for penetration.

A third alternative for the woman, while she is in this sitting-in-the-lap position, is to lower one leg. The other leg remains over his hip. The man then can penetrate her vagina.

One more option is to have the man lie on his back, with the woman straddling him. She takes his penis and inserts it inside her. Then she may lean forward and rest her torso on his chest.

If you are not successful at first, keep trying. Practicing is a lot of fun and becomes a very shared experience. In the event that the man is unable to penetrate, keep the penis against the inner lips of the vagina, and linger in that position instead. You will be touching and the warmth will be equally apparent.

As you both breathe quietly and touch gently, maintain the sexual ebb and flow, rising and falling. You may experience a sexual rippling throughout your body, but if you are not being actively stimulated the rippling will fade for a time and then reappear. Being passive together alleviates the urgency for orgasm and supports the continued closeness. Stay focused, keep your eyes closed, and take your pleasure from caresses as you prepare to leave this quiet stage of penetration.

The building of sexual feeling is gradual during this hour, reaching a level that is often quite intense. Some people liken it to the feeling immediately following orgasm when there may be minimal movement but the nerve endings are tingling and highly responsive. Quiet penetration is particularly valuable at times when thrusting is desired but is unrealistic for one reason or another. Aches and pains are sometimes aggravated by movement but may be soothed by caressing and physical closeness. This further provides time to be intimate without performance goals or unreasonable expectations; a time to touch one another without dissipating the energy through orgasmic response.

Quiet penetration is a position suitable to sleeping, and it is not uncommon for lovers to fall asleep while still entwined. If they remain quiet throughout the night, they may find themselves still connected upon awakening. Sometimes it is difficult to discern whether active intercourse has actually occurred, but the feeling is warm and loving nonetheless.

As always, follow your own pathway. You may find other sexual positions that work equally as well as the ones suggested. Experiment with breathing techniques such as breathing in the same rhythm or breathing alternately. Notice the difference, if any, in your response and excitation when you change breathing patterns.

One resourceful couple found a unique way of communicating during this exercise.

"We both know Morse code, and we've found we can talk to each other during quiet penetration by contracting the love muscles to spell out messages. It's fantastic exercise for the PC, and it's a kind of close communication we've never felt before."

Now that you have experienced a high level of sensitivity while intimately joined, it is appropriate to progress to intercourse. Begin with easy thrusting at first, slowly building sexual tension and excitement.

There are many positions suitable to this movement in addition to the missionary and rear entry positions. With the man lying on his back, the woman can straddle him and insert his penis. Balancing herself on her hands, she can slide up and down on his penis, controlling not only the depth of his penetration but also the pace of his thrusting. The effect is highly stimulating. Or the two lovers can sit facing one another, the woman's thighs over the man's, joined at the genitals. They can push toward and pull away from each other, and in so doing will be aware of the warmth and wetness between them.

The urgency to let go and thrust wildly may be strong, but practice the delay techniques you have

learned. Rest and study what is happening to both of you before riding the crest again. This will be a different feeling from the rapid, active kind of lovemaking.

There is a seemingly basic contradiction inherent in intercourse. While it is certainly an act based on sharing and mutuality, as orgasm becomes imminent it becomes a separate and self-serving experience. No one else is having the sensations you are, and no one else can accompany you on your ascent to climax. Following orgasm, you and your lover gradually fuse once more and the feeling of oneness returns.

Achieving simultaneous orgasm, or coming together, has been idealized as the ultimate in sexual bonding. There is really no such thing as coming together. You are totally absorbed in your own pleasure when you are in the ecstasy of your orgasm. You are reacting to your passion, and you are unable to share that response with anyone. It is no less loving to reach orgasm before your partner does. Lovemaking is not validated by the synchronization of orgasms. It is a process of give and take, with sensitivity and caring.

For many reasons, the outcome of your sexual encounter will vary from time to time. The techniques used, the physical and mental state of the lovers, the time of the month, the climate and time of day, the environment, and motivation are a few of the variables that affect the sex experience. The important issue is to enjoy all your pleasure as it happens, without looking ahead to a goal.

An orgasm is not a necessary ending to your lovemaking. There may be times when you tire yourselves from being active and your preference is to fall asleep without reaching climax. It may be an inopportune time to be orgasmic, for whatever reason, and there is absolutely nothing wrong with that. There is no right or wrong outcome to intercourse. To be satiated from the thrusting and caressing without orgasm does not indicate an underactive libido, nor is it in any way abnormal. Every time you make love it changes, because you are constantly changing and adjusting to each other's feeling and desires. Trust your body.

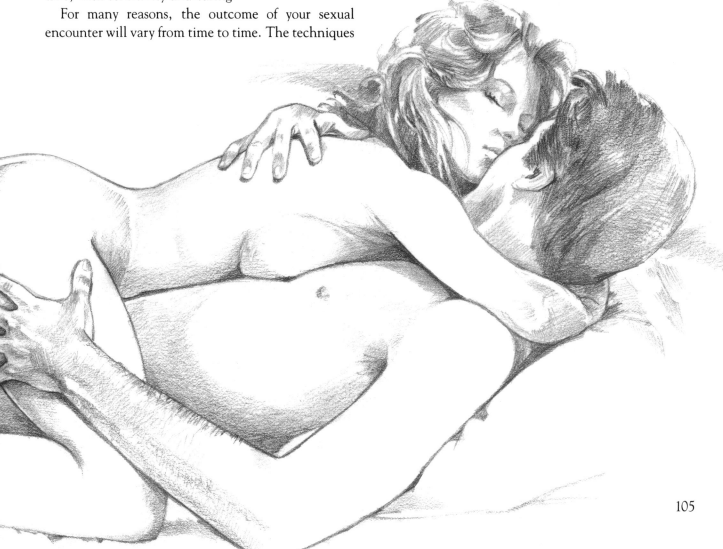

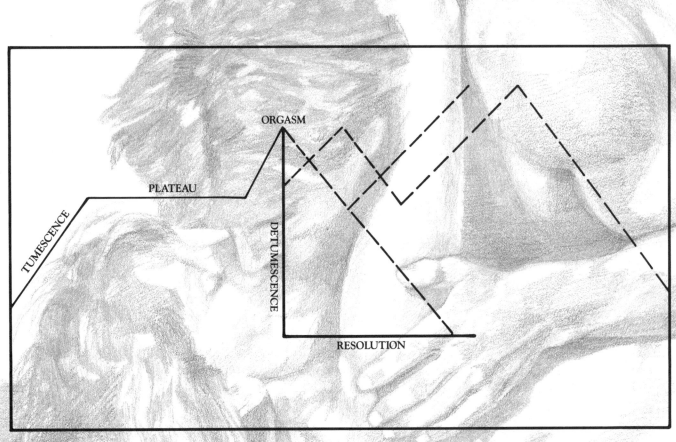

ORGASM

PLATEAU

TUMESCENCE

DETUMESCENCE

RESOLUTION

MASTERS & JOHNSON HUMAN SEXUAL RESPONSE CHART

We mentioned the separation process that occurs between you and your partner at the time of orgasm, as you each have your own orgasmic experience. There may be times when the separation factor fuses instead into mutual sexual energy. It sometimes becomes difficult to determine who is penetrating and who is being penetrated. As the bodies surrender to each other they stay connected in their ascent to orgasm.

This would seem to contradict the notion that we experience orgasm in a singular mode every time. There are no limits to what is possible. Whatever and how-ever you experience your sexuality is your reality as you know it. Sex need never become boring.

For some lovers, orgasm means the diminishing of sexual desire and therefore an end to the activity. For others, it is the catalyst for desiring further stimulation and more orgasms. Understanding your personal response to orgasm is important. If you know that your interest in satisfying your partner decreases with climax, then you might want to avoid orgasm until such time as you both mutually agree upon. Be attentive to your body and to your particular need.

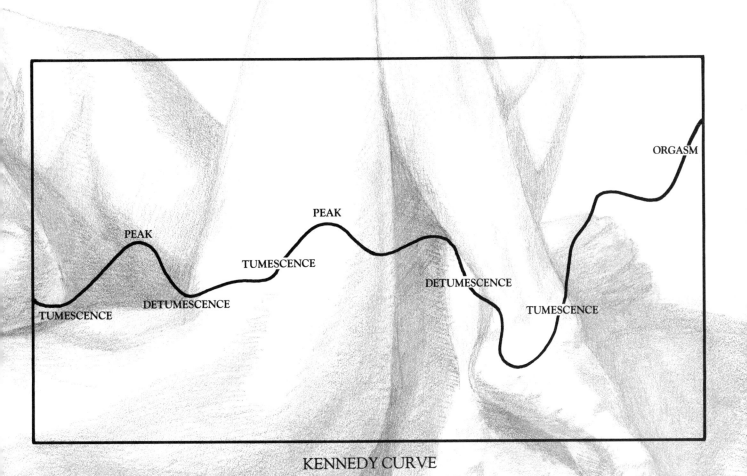

PEAK

PEAK

ORGASM

TUMESCENCE

TUMESCENCE

TUMESCENCE

DETUMESCENCE

DETUMESCENCE

TUMESCENCE

KENNEDY CURVE

According to the Masters and Johnson Curve of Human Sexual Response, we begin our orgasmic climb in a state of tumescence, or excitation. A point is reached at which the urgency is unbearably exciting and time seems suspended. That is called the plateau stage. When it becomes so intense that you cannot control it, you go into orgasm. After the orgasm you begin to cool down, or detumesce. When your sexual organs return to their original state of relaxation, this is the resolution phase.

The Kennedy Curve measures the orgasmic response a bit differently. You become excited and you reach a peak. You cool down for a bit and then turn on again and peak once more. This process is unpredictable and the peaks may be big or small, weak or strong. But they are repeated until, if you stay with it, you eventually surrender to a powerful peak and reach climax. It is much like the waves of the ocean, rolling in and then out again, building and releasing sexual tension and energy, and then one giant wave comes along and knocks you over. Sexually speaking, that is your orgasm. You then experience a kind of euphoria, which the

French call "petit mort," or little death.

The fun of intercourse is drawing from all your resources and applying your knowledge to lovemaking. Kissing is as much a part of making love as is caressing with your hands. Oral sex can be alternated with intercourse, especially at a time when you want a change from thrusting. Though the concentration may be on the genitals, stimulate other places on the body that you and your lover have experienced as being sensually and sexually responsive. If the man is lying on top of the woman, she can reach up and caress his face and back. If the man is penetrating the woman from a rear entry position, his hands are free to caress her in many places. In the spoon position, the man can touch the woman's breasts and clitoris to provide additional stimulus while still inside her. If both lovers are sitting up facing one another, they are able to mutually hold and caress each other all over.

Anal penetration is another option, but do not have vaginal intercourse after anal penetration without first washing the penis thoroughly. Always use a lubricant as the anal opening is generally smaller and more delicate than the vaginal entrance. Penetrate slowly, without force, and let the sphincter relax to permit comfortable entry.

In your lovemaking, free all your erotic impulses. Taste the genital juices, anoint each other's bodies with ejaculate, play with pubic hair, suck on toes, and whatever else you desire. There is no limit to the entertainment that sexual touching can provide.

The absence of talking in prior exercises gave you a chance to learn about your own sexuality without the distraction of dialogue and intellect. You did not verbally affirm or deny to your partner whether you enjoyed yourself, were satisfied, or had plans to do it again. You were left to your enjoyment and fulfillment.

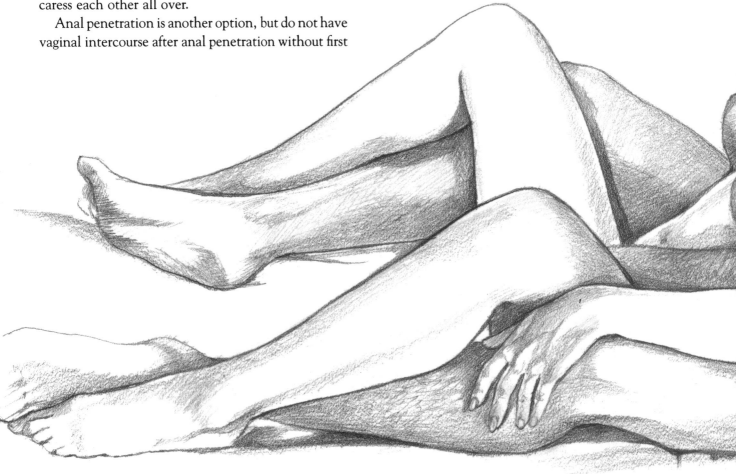

You were encouraged to be selfish.

Silent lovemaking does have its advantages, especially while you are learning concentration, but there is a need for all of us to be heard, and intercourse is a time when sounds are welcomed. During stages of excitation you might want to moan, groan, sigh, pant, giggle, cry, whimper, cough, hum, scream, or grunt. These sounds are not only natural during lovemaking, but are helpful in generating sexual feelings and releasing energy. Your sounds will often excite your partner, and before long you are both creating your own very special love sonata.

Intercourse also lends itself to talking. You may want to let your partner know how and what you are feeling. Discuss changing positions or trying something new. Let each other know when you are are close to orgasm. Do not hesitate to communicate discomfort; but remember that a negative exchange such as a complaint can be the quickest road to premature ejaculation, impotence, or immediate loss of desire. Good feelings are essential to a good lovemaking experience.

Immediately following intercourse most lovers experience feelings of peacefulness and satisfaction. We call this time *afterplay*, and you are encouraged to make full use of it. It can be the sweetest time of all, as you lie in each other's arms, holding and touching. You might even fall asleep. Some people claim feelings of high energy after intercourse, whereas others feel spent. The breathing coming down from intercourse may be labored and rapid, gradually becoming slow and even. Responses change each time. Trust your body and your instincts. You may just want to express your feelings about each other, or you may want to listen to the quiet, and focus inside yourself, almost like a meditative state. This is a perfect time to quietly settle a problem. It is impossible to fight while love feelings still glow. Whatever it is you each need from this time, take it in abundance.

You will discover for yourself that afterplay allows you time for expression to complete the total experience. Then when you do separate from your lover, you will feel prepared to make that separation. As you began, so shall you complete, gently and lovingly.

TOUCHING IS ITS OWN REWARD

12

Touching
is a
need belonging
to all
of us and
that
need is
everlasting

The setting was a nursing home for the elderly. Some of the residents were infirm, but others had just grown old. They talked together, ate together, complained together, and loved together. Friendships formed and sometimes replaced actual family relationships. They watched each other come and go, sometimes never to return. The old people were troopers, though, understanding that they were all there on borrowed time. At least that is what they were told by the media, by the doctors, and by their families. Most of them knew that every minute counted. They took very little for granted. Some attempted to make up for lost time.

It was dinner hour and all the senior citizens were assembled in the dining room. Someone noticed that two people were missing from the group—a man and a woman, unrelated to each other but friends.

The alert spread quickly throughout the home, and a search began. All the rooms and beds were empty, the kitchen deserted, and the outdoor patio bare. A nurse checked to see if any medication was missing from the storage closet, and upon opening the door screamed at what she uncovered. She found the man and woman. They were embracing each other in silence.

She quickly called for security. The two *sex offenders* were separated and escorted to their rooms. Families were called, conferences held, and doctors consulted. The consensus was that the two promiscuous culprits should not be allowed further contact. They were a disgrace to their community.

Humiliated and confused, frightened and guilt ridden, the two rapidly withdrew from friends and family. Within weeks of the crime, they both died. Their friends cried. So did their families. But no amount of tears could undo the tragedy.

The need for touching does not exclude the elderly. While the skin of an older person may be aesthetically less appealing because of wrinkles, spotting, and dryness, the human being inside the skin craves touching more than ever.

It is not uncommon for aging persons who never had any interest in having a pet earlier in life to sublimate their tactile needs in later years through an animal. A warm, snuggling kitten or a fun-loving puppy often replaces the absence of human contact.

One day we all hope to be members of the senior community, equally craving a hug or caress. Though our sexual activity may decrease or end completely, our desire to be sensually active and appealing will remain very much alive. We too shall look for encouragement and acknowledgment through loving hands and kind embraces. Our ability to give and receive tactile pleasure will then become life-sustaining, as well as gratifying. Touching is a need belonging to us all, and that need is everlasting.

"A thirty-year-old masseur was a product of touch starvation. He had no recollection of ever having been touched by his parents or friends. He was withdrawn,

shy around girls, afraid he was homosexual, and lived a life of loneliness and despair. His need for tactile stimulation became obsessive.

"But he was more fortunate than some. A friend of his was studying massage and asked the young man if he would volunteer for a practice session. From the moment he was touched, he knew that he had found his path at last. He began to understand how, by giving pleasure to others, he could receive pleasure for himself. He had discovered the basic principle of touching for pleasure."

In this program we have shown you, in a fundamental way, how to eliminate touch starvation from your world. Your success in attaining fulfillment will depend largely on your commitment to the value of touching, and to your responsibility for your own needs, wants, and gratification.

Return to the hand caress. As you go through the process once more, notice the immeasurable difference in the depth of your feeling and response. Having come full circle, this is a significant closing exercise, since it was the very first one you practiced. Your ability to concentrate and to feel has changed considerably. Your hand, or the hand you caress, takes on another dimension; the sensations are strong and well-defined.

Make every effort to get out of focus, by thinking about problems at work, about unpaid bills or the last book you read. Try to be oblivious to touching or being touched. It is no longer easy to do. You have learned how to ignore noise and distraction, making it nearly

TOUCHING IS
ITS OWN REWARD

impossible to address extraneous anxiety and interference. This is good. You understand how to keep intellect and feeling separate.

It is seldom necessary to resort to prescribed exercises as a way of being touched. Now that you have completed your study, the steps in this program are available merely as a reminder and refresher. Look all around you as well as within for sources of pleasuring.

Have you ever noticed how your clothes touch your body? Tight clothes embrace you; looser-fitting garments glide over your skin, giving intermittent caresses. Silk and satin feel different from flannel and wool. Which one feels best against your body? Take your pleasure where you find it. It belongs to you.

The next time you join your children in front of the television, sit close, stroking their hair or caressing their backs. This will not be a distraction. A bonding is maintained despite their attention elsewhere when you musingly touch for pleasure.

With a mate it is not necessary to reserve touching for private and secluded moments. Sit side by side in a restaurant, slightly touching, feeling the warmth between your bodies. Hold hands in the movies. Walk arm in arm along the beach. Hug in the kitchen. Take a bubble bath together and talk over the events of the day. Rub lotion on each other at bedtime. And most of all, go to sleep with your hands or bodies touching, establishing a close physical connection.

Touching is a gift of self. It is a universal language of love. Whether you caress passionately or touch gently, you are using the skin as a conductor of feeling. You are speaking without words. In time, touching becomes a way of life, central to all you do.

So many of our years are spent searching outside ourselves for pleasure, waiting for it to come to us. We need to look inside, to be the navigators of our own individual course. While we contemplate lifelong goals and monetary gain, let us not overlook the real treasures that reside within each of us. Regardless of income, education, or title, we all have the capacity for pleasure.

Unlike a contest promising a prize at the finish line, the value of touching for pleasure is in doing each and every step. Touching is its own reward.

TOUCHING IS
ITS OWN REWARD

SAFER CHOICES

A Guide to Minimizing the Risk of Contracting Sexually Transmitted Diseases.

By Susan Perry

The desire to touch and be touched is one of the most basic urges felt by humans. That is one reason why so many men and women enter physical relationships with people they barely know, ignoring warnings about sexually transmitted diseases (STD's). In fact, even in today's climate of fear about AIDS, a disease that is nearly always fatal, a certain percentage of men and women act as though sex were as safe as it used to be. But it is not.

AIDS is not the only STD, but it is certainly the most frightening one. In the past few years it has been spreading in epidemic proportions among members of certain high risk groups. However, experts are sharply divided as to how high the risk of sex is for the average heterosexual.

Some experts believe that any form of intimate contact can lead to the passing of viruses from an infected person to his or her partner. The AIDS virus may hide in the affected person's system for years before any symptoms show up, so that it is indeed possible for someone to be carrying the virus without knowing it.

One study showed that among a group of heterosexuals with multiple partners, none of whom had other known risk factors, seven percent of the women and five percent of the men tested positive for carrying antibodies to the AIDS virus. This means that five to seven percent of this particular group could be spreading the AIDS virus to a wider population.

Other experts, however, believe that if you choose your partner carefully, and reliable condoms are worn, you can engage in sexual intercourse with relative safety. For example, a recent report by two San Francisco researchers, published in *The Journal of the American Medical Association,* states that the chance of catching the AIDS virus from a single act of hetero-

sexual intercourse with an infected partner is one in 500 if no condom is used. But if you have sex with a low-risk partner who has been tested and found free of the virus, and you use a condom, the odds you will catch the virus are reduced to only one in five billion.

Obviously, these odds are much more comforting. Yet, even so, other venereal diseases besides AIDS could be putting you at risk every time you have sex. For example, herpes simplex is widespread and incurable, and though not life-threatening, it can be a persistent nuisance. There is no foolproof way to be sure your partner is free of herpes, except by means of a blood test.

Syphilis is a very serious, chronic venereal disease which is transmitted through contact with infected areas of the skin. Its initial symptoms are painless and only show up briefly weeks after infection, so very often those infected are not even aware they are carriers. Antibiotics are used to treat syphilis, but if untreated, damage to the nervous system or heart can show up years later. The current nationwide rise in cases of syphilis is particularly worrisome because there is some evidence that syphilis may heighten a person's risk of infection with AIDS. A simple blood test is used to diagnose syphilis.

Gonorrhea is the most common venereal disease. The disease is transmitted sexually, and often symptoms in women are slight: painful urination and slight discharge. It, too, can be diagnosed by medical tests, and treated with drugs. If left untreated, it can affect future pregnancies and cause other damage.

Chlamydia is also extremely common these days, with symptoms similar to those of gonorrhea, but usually milder. After diagnosis, antibiotics are used to cure the disease. As with all sexually transmitted diseases, it is important to refrain from sexual activity until the infection is completely cured.

Now you have an idea what the risks are. Still, you need more information to make safer sexual choices. Who is high risk? How does the AIDS test work and when do you need one? When do you need a condom, and what kinds are best? And how do you deal with all these variables in the heat of the moment without either alienating a potential partner or dampening your own sexual mood?

First of all, it should go without saying that it is not very safe to have sex with total strangers. A stranger is someone you meet in a singles bar, the supermarket, or through an ad in a singles publication, with whom you have no friends in common. If you do not take time to get to know the person quite well, there is really no way you can be sure they are being completely honest with you.

Still, by questioning a prospective sex partner with the important risk factors in mind, you can certainly lessen your chances of contracting AIDS or another venereal disease. You need to be aware that the riskiest groups to avoid are homosexual or bisexual men and intravenous drug users from major metropolitan areas, and hemophiliacs. Lower risks are involved with homosexual or bisexual men and drug users from smaller towns, prostitutes, heterosexuals from Haiti and Africa, and recipients of multiple blood transfusions in the early 1980's. And, of course, you want to avoid anyone who suspects they may be infected with *any* venereal disease, especially if a previous partner of theirs has come down with an infection.

So when you meet a new person with whom you would like to have a sexual relationship, try to get to know something about their present and past sexual history. Obviously, there is no subtle way to ask these personal questions, but you can use a certain amount of tact. For example, you might say something like this:

"I'm really attracted to you and I'd very much like to get closer, but with all this scare about AIDS and other diseases, I'm kind of worried. If I could ask you some questions first, it would put my mind at ease and I could relax with you."

Once your partner understands that you are insisting on openness and honesty about his past sexual experiences, you can go ahead and ask the following questions:

"Have you ever had a same-sex experience? Do you use drugs? What kind and how do you take them?"

It would be exceedingly risky to have sex with someone who is homosexual. You will also want to find out if he is a hemophiliac, or is from Haiti or Africa. Taking the AIDS test together is just good sense in these cases.

Age can also be a factor to consider, as older people who have not been dating for many years may be safer than young people who date a lot. Ask: "How long has it been since you dated last? How often do you date per month? Do you usually have sex right away or after knowing the person for a certain length of time?"

If they seem to be "swingers," or people who enjoy sexual relationships with large numbers of people regardless of gender, you're certainly increasing your own risk of contracting a disease if you get physically involved. Ask: "Where do you meet most of your sexual partners? Have you ever switched partners with another couple? Have you ever made love to more than one person at a time? When you are dating someone, are you sexually monogamous?"

You *can* take precautions that will swing the odds greatly in your favor, but remember, there is no such thing as totally "safe sex" outside of a long-term monogamous relationship that has been going on for many years.

One couple in their 30's, even though they have been completely monogamous for more than five years, still cannot be absolutely sure they are in the clear. Statistics say that the latency period for the AIDS virus can be as long as eight to ten years. Each member of this couple had been involved with one or more partners who had themselves previously slept with 100 or so others, so occasionally, this couple wonders if any of their ex-lovers was carrying the virus. Since it has been said that when you sleep with someone, you are sleeping with all of their former lovers also, they indeed have at least *some* reason to worry.

A particular source of concern to this couple is that one of the husband's previous lovers had been married to a man who turned out to be homosexual. It is especially these "cross-over" relationships that contribute to the spread of AIDS. It has also been noted that many more people than admit it, especially men, have been involved with a member of their own sex.

As recently as five to ten years ago, before most people were aware of the seriousness of AIDS, other sexually transmitted diseases made sex with strangers risky. One 27-year-old woman who dated widely about six years ago became very concerned when she found out that one of her lovers was also having sexual relationships with a number of other women at the same time. In spite of her fear of herpes, however, she continued to date him. Still, every time they got together, she questioned him about his recent activities. And he would always answer, "Oh no, not another herpes conversation."

Actually, her friend was one of those who feel themselves to be invulnerable to catching sexual diseases. In fact, he said, "Once I made love to a woman who admitted she had herpes. She wasn't having an outbreak at the time, and anyway, it was kind of exciting taking that risk."

If you do not find that type of risk-taking exciting, you will want to avoid people who do. And if you cannot imagine yourself discussing such intimate topics with a new acquaintance, it does not make much sense to put your health and perhaps life in their hands by agreeing to sexual intercourse at an early stage of the relationship.

Another form of risk-taking is trusting your intuition blindly. A 40-year-old woman who teaches parent education classes is typical.

"I don't think about getting AIDS or other diseases," she says. "I might pick up someone and go to bed with him without protection. I choose people intuitively. To me, he would not be just a person I picked up off the street, but a particular human being I feel safe with, even if I've just met him for the first time."

One study showed that this sort of nonchalance is quite widespread. When she was asked how she dealt with the prospect of AIDS when sleeping with men she did not know well, one 24-year-old woman said, "It can't happen to me." Do not make the mistake of believing you are not at risk.

The only way you can be certain your partner does not have a sexually transmitted disease is by asking him to go to a doctor or medical clinic and have appropriate tests. The AIDS virus can only be detected with a special antibody test. If both partners' test results show them to be free of the virus, they then need to wait six months before taking the test again. This is to exclude the cases in which the initial test occurs too soon after infection for detectable quantities of antibody to have developed. Of course, if you can be absolutely certain your partner has had no other partners for six months before you met, only one test would be necessary.

Once you've qualified a potential lover by means of some careful questioning and perhaps testing, there are some specific things you can do to protect yourself.

Ideally, after an AIDS test, you and your partner should not engage in sexual activity with each other or with anyone else during the six-month waiting period. Since this is asking too much restraint for most people, the next safest course is to use condoms consistently during that period between tests, whether for vaginal intercourse or fellatio.

As far as AIDS is concerned, anal sex is the riskiest type of sexual activity. You will want to avoid it, then, if your partner's health status is at all unclear, if he or she has not been tested yet, and during the period between the first and second tests.

Of course, almost nothing in modern life is 100 percent safe. We all know that simply riding in a car is fairly risky. Still, in a car, you wear a seat belt to lessen your risk and improve your odds of survival in case of accident. In the same way, when you insist that your partner wear a condom, you are taking care of yourself and greatly reducing your chances of becoming ill.

So until something better comes along, condoms must be your choice of protection against sexually transmitted diseases, including gonorrhea, syphilis, herpes simplex, chlamydia, and AIDS. Though some researchers argue that condoms have not been proven to provide foolproof protection against these viruses, most experts insist they are far better than not using any protection at all.

Unfortunately, recent tests have shown that 12 percent of the condoms made in the United States and 21 percent of those made in other countries failed. These are laboratory tests of water-leakage under pressure, and do not exactly apply to humans during sexual intercourse, but at least it gives you some idea. Another important factor to consider is that latex condoms offer more protection than those made of natural membranes, like lamb cecum. So when choosing condoms, it would be safest to stick with U.S.-made latex brands.

One variable which *is* under your control is how you use condoms. You must use them each time you have sexual intercourse, put them on before any genital contact takes place, and you must completely unroll the condom. Problems can occur if you use an oil-based lubricant that weakens latex, if you don't use enough lubrication, or if you don't leave enough space at the tip of the condom for the ejaculate.

Lately, more and more women have been going into drugstores and buying their own condoms, just so they'll be prepared. A 37-year-old children's book author describes how she prepared for a first date: "I chose a package of condoms, exactly the right kind you're supposed to use—the American-made latex ones—and took them home. I even told my date about it, so he would know how important my health is to me. But, and this is so dumb, when we finally ended up in bed, I didn't bother to get them from my purse."

This does not have to happen to you. The use of condoms can be incorporated into the act of lovemaking so that it is less of an interruption. It is exciting for a man to have his penis handled by a woman, so ask him if you can help put the condom on him. Or if you feel shy about this, ask your partner to show you how to do it the first time.

No woman who cares about her health and safety minds when a man wants to use a condom. One 17-year-old boy planning his first sexual encounter said, "I think she's on the pill so we don't have to worry about birth control. So won't she be angry or insulted if I ask to use a condom?"

The odds are a sexually active teenage girl will not be upset if a boy wants to use a condom. The condom should be brought out without asking, by either partner, just as a matter of course. It is, after all, for the protection of both parties.

A 47-year-old family counselor began dating again after the breakup of a lengthy relationship. She met a man with whom she might have a satisfying relationship, except for one thing. They were both afraid of contracting AIDS. They talked about having the AIDS test, but both of them put it off. Meanwhile, they spent time together with no physical contact whatsoever.

It is too bad neither of them knew ways of being sensual with each other without indulging in sexual intercourse. For example, look back over the previous chapters of this book. Hand, foot, and full body massages are delightful ways to relate to another person without necessarily having to lead to intercourse. If either or both of you want to have orgasms, you can masturbate yourselves or each other. Your partner might consider using a vibrator on you if his fear of AIDS causes him to be uneasy about coming into contact with your bodily fluids.

Many people very much enjoy the sensual pleasures of taking a shower together. Since the intimacy of this activity, combined with slippery, soapy touching, may lead to a desire for sexual satisfaction, you might allow your partner to use a hand-held shower sprayer on you to bring you to orgasm. And he can easily bring himself to orgasm while watching you.

The key to alternative methods of sexual relating is to choose a partner whom you can trust. Trust makes it so much easier to relax with a person, and then it is not a problem to touch yourself in his presence. In fact, many men claim to become very excited when a woman is free enough to masturbate herself while he watches. One 37-year-old lawyer says he counts among his favorite sexual experiences the times he has masturbated to orgasm while kneeling over his partner. At the same time, he manipulates her or she brings herself to orgasm by hand or with a vibrator.

Be aware, however, that unless your partner has very little chance of carrying a virus or infection, it is not completely safe for his ejaculate to come in contact with your skin. The AIDS virus can enter your body if you have even the tiniest cut. The mouth is particularly prone to having unnoticed abrasions and cuts, and that is why it may be dangerous to have oral sex with a partner who has not yet passed an AIDS test.

If you do perform fellatio on your partner, remember that even if you withdraw before he ejaculates, some fluid still enters your mouth. Therefore, it is wise to use a condom even for fellatio. This idea may seem strange at first, but it is often done successfully by women who are concerned about their health and safety.

Another option for those who want to experience sexual pleasures together without the risk of sexual intercourse is to use fantasy as a springboard. For example, "phone sex" is commonly used by lovers who must be separated for any length of time. It can just as easily be used by new partners. Simply call up your partner, get comfortable, and begin masturbating while you both talk about what you are doing or would like to do sexually. The more audibly creative you are, the better.

As you can see, by using your imagination as well as your body, you *can* find ways to get around the riskiness of sex. You do not have to forego the joys of touching for pleasure. If you simply remember to make careful sexual choices, you will be giving yourself the gift of relaxed, enjoyable, and *safe* relationships.

Brecher, Edward M. *Love, Sex, and Aging.* Boston: Little, Brown and Co., 1984

Hartman, Dr. William, and Marilyn Fithian. *Any Man Can.* New York: St. Martin's Press, 1984

Ladas, Alice Kahn, Beverly Whipple, and John D. Perry. *The G Spot.* New York: Dell Publishing Co., 1982

LeBoyer, Frederick. *Loving Hands.* New York: Alfred A. Knopf, 1979

Masters, William H., and Virginia E. Johnson. *Human Sexual Inadequacy.* Boston: Little, Brown and Co., 1982

Montagu, Ashley. *Touching.* New York: Harper and Row Publishers, 1971

Morris, Desmond. *Intimate Behaviour.* New York: Random House, 1971

Ribble, Margaret A. *The Rights of Infants.* New York and London: Columbia University Press, 1965

Rosenberg, Jack L. *Total Orgasm.* New York: Random House, 1973

Rossi, William A. *The Sex Life of the Foot and Shoe.* New York: Ballantine Books, 1976

Stewart, Jessica. *The Complete Manual of Sexual Positions.* Chatsworth: Media Press, 1983

Winter, Ruth. "How People React to Your Touch." *Science Digest.* March 1976

"G-Spot Found in Autopsy Exams." *Forum Magazine.* July 1983

THE CRITICS AND PROFESSIONALS COMMENT ON

TOUCHING FOR PLEASURE

THE MALE PARTNER:

". . . Kennedy is a pioneer sex surrogate who draws on her own experience with dysfunctional patients to explain those problems that tend to concern men regarding sex."[7]

BODY IMAGE:

". . . you will focus on the positive parts of your body without self-consciousness in order to accept yourself the way you are."[8]

TOUCHING AND THE PHYSICALLY DISABLED:

". . . TOUCHING FOR PLEASURE is sensitively written and emphasizes the comprehensive role and enormous value of touch . . . People with disabilities are 'handled' with greater frequency than able-bodied persons and touch becomes a very complex and often altered issue . . . I have used this book in conjunction with counseling injured individuals and their partners as well as persons with congenital disabilities. The response has been positive. Thank you for a sensible and sensitive contribution."[9]

7) Warren Chatterly, ON THE SCENE; 8) March; 9) Sandra S. Cole, Professor, Dept. of Physical Medicine and Rehabilitation, University of Michigan.